Simple 1-2-3™
Slow Cooker

pil

Publications International, Ltd.

Favorite Brand Name Recipes at www.fbnr.com

Pictured on the front cover: Italian-Style Pot Roast *(page 26)*.
Pictured on the back cover *(counterclockwise from top):* Caribbean Sweet Potato & Bean Stew *(page 141)*, Easy Homemade Barbecue *(page 56)* and Italian-Style Sausage with Rice *(page 44)*.

The publisher would like to thank Reckitt Benckiser Inc. for the use of their recipes in this publication.

Ingredient photography by Shaughnessy MacDonald, Inc.

ISBN: 1-4127-2176-8

Library of Congress Control Number: 2004115116

Manufactured in China.

8 7 6 5 4 3 2 1

Contents

Starters

Festive Bacon & Cheese Dip

2 packages (8 ounces each) cream cheese, cut into cubes

4 cups (16 ounces) shredded Colby-Jack cheese

1 cup half-and-half

2 tablespoons prepared mustard

1 tablespoon chopped onion

2 teaspoons Worcestershire sauce

½ teaspoon salt

¼ teaspoon hot pepper sauce

1 pound bacon, crisp-cooked and crumbled

1. Combine cream cheese, Colby-Jack cheese, half-and-half, mustard, onion, Worcestershire sauce, salt and hot pepper sauce in slow cooker.

2. Cover; cook, stirring occasionally, on LOW 1 hour or until cheese melts.

3. Stir in bacon; adjust seasonings. Serve with crusty bread or vegetable dippers.

Makes about 4 cups dip

Mulled Apple Cider

2 quarts apple cider or
   juice
¼ cup packed light brown
   sugar
1 square (8 inches) double-
   thickness cheesecloth
8 allspice berries
4 cinnamon sticks, broken
   into halves
12 whole cloves
1 large orange
   Additional cinnamon
   sticks (optional)

1. Combine apple cider and brown sugar in slow cooker. Rinse cheesecloth; squeeze out water. Wrap allspice berries and cinnamon stick halves in cheesecloth; tie securely with cotton string or strip of cheesecloth. Stick cloves randomly into orange; cut orange into quarters. Place spice bag and orange quarters in cider mixture.

2. Cover; cook on HIGH 2½ to 3 hours.

3. Once cooked, cider may be turned to LOW and kept warm up to 3 additional hours. Remove and discard spice bag and orange before serving. Ladle cider into mugs; garnish with additional cinnamon sticks, if desired.

Makes 10 servings

Tip: To make inserting cloves into the orange a little easier, first pierce the orange skin with the point of wooden skewer. Remove the skewer and insert a clove.

Creamy Artichoke-Parmesan Dip

1. Combine artichokes, cheeses, mayonnaise, onion, oregano and garlic powder in slow cooker; mix well.

2. Cover; cook on LOW 2 hours.

3. Meanwhile, cut pita breads into wedges. Arrange pita breads and vegetables on platter; serve with warm dip.

Makes 4 cups dip

2 cans (14 ounces each) artichoke hearts, drained and chopped
2 cups (8 ounces) shredded mozzarella cheese
1½ cups grated Parmesan cheese
1½ cups mayonnaise
½ cup finely chopped onion
½ teaspoon dried oregano
¼ teaspoon garlic powder
4 pita breads
Assorted cut-up vegetables

Honey-Mustard Chicken Wings

3 pounds chicken wings
1 teaspoon salt
1 teaspoon black pepper
½ cup honey
½ cup barbecue sauce
2 tablespoons spicy brown
   mustard
1 clove garlic, minced
3 to 4 thin lemon slices

1. Rinse chicken and pat dry. Cut off wing tips; discard. Cut each wing at joint to make two pieces. Sprinkle salt and pepper on both sides of chicken. Place wing pieces on broiler rack. Broil 4 to 5 inches from heat about 10 minutes, turning halfway through cooking time. Place broiled chicken wings in slow cooker.

2. Combine honey, barbecue sauce, mustard and garlic in small bowl; mix well. Pour sauce over chicken wings. Top with lemon slices. Cover; cook on LOW 4 to 5 hours.

3. Remove and discard lemon slices. Serve wings with sauce.

Makes about 24 appetizers

Chunky Pinto Bean Dip

1. Combine beans, tomatoes, onion, salsa, oil, garlic, coriander and cumin in slow cooker.

2. Cover; cook on LOW 5 to 6 hours or until onion is tender.

3. Partially mash bean mixture with potato masher. Stir in cheese and cilantro. Serve at room temperature with chips and vegetables.

Makes about 5 cups dip

2 cans (15 ounces each) pinto beans, rinsed and drained
1 can (14½ ounces) diced tomatoes with green chilies
1 cup chopped onion
⅔ cup chunky salsa
1 tablespoon vegetable oil
1½ teaspoons minced garlic
1 teaspoon ground coriander
1 teaspoon ground cumin
1½ cups (6 ounces) shredded Mexican cheese blend
¼ cup chopped cilantro
Blue corn or other tortilla chips
Assorted raw vegetables

Chai Tea

2 quarts (8 cups) water
8 bags black tea
¾ cup sugar*
16 whole cloves
16 whole cardamom seeds,
    pods removed
5 cinnamon sticks
8 slices fresh ginger
1 cup milk

*Chai Tea is typically a sweet drink.
For less sweet tea, reduce sugar to
½ cup.

1. Combine water, tea, sugar, cloves, cardamom, cinnamon and ginger in slow cooker. Cover; cook on HIGH 2 to 2½ hours.

2. Strain mixture; discard solids. (At this point, tea may be covered and refrigerated up to 3 days).

3. Stir in milk just before serving. Serve warm or chilled.

Makes 8 to 10 servings

Maple-Glazed Meatballs

1. Combine ketchup, maple syrup, soy sauce, tapioca, allspice and mustard in slow cooker.

2. Partially thaw and separate meatballs. Carefully stir meatballs and pineapple chunks into ketchup mixture.

3. Cover; cook on LOW 5 to 6 hours. Stir before serving. Serve with cocktail picks.   *Makes about 48 meatballs*

Variation: Serve over hot cooked rice for an entrée.

1½ cups ketchup
  1 cup maple syrup or maple-flavored syrup
  ⅓ cup reduced-sodium soy sauce
  1 tablespoon quick-cooking tapioca
1½ teaspoons ground allspice
  1 teaspoon dry mustard
  2 packages (about 16 ounces each) frozen fully-cooked meatballs
  1 can (20 ounces) pineapple chunks in juice, drained

Easy Taco Dip

½ **pound ground beef chuck**
1 **cup frozen corn**
½ **cup chopped onion**
½ **cup salsa**
½ **cup mild taco sauce**
1 **can (4 ounces) diced mild green chilies**
1 **can (4 ounces) sliced ripe olives, drained**
1 **cup (4 ounces) shredded Mexican cheese blend**
Tortilla chips
Sour cream

1. Brown ground beef in large nonstick skillet over medium-high heat, stirring to separate meat. Drain and discard fat. Spoon into slow cooker.

2. Add corn, onion, salsa, taco sauce, chilies and olives to slow cooker; mix well. Cover; cook on LOW 2 to 4 hours.

3. Stir in cheese just before serving. Serve with tortilla chips and sour cream.

Makes about 3 cups dip

Tip: To keep this dip hot through your entire party, simply leave it in the slow cooker on LOW.

Starters

Brats in Beer

1. Combine bratwurst, beer, onion, brown sugar and vinegar in slow cooker.

2. Cover; cook on LOW 4 to 5 hours.

3. Remove bratwurst from cooking liquid. Cut into ½-inch-thick slices. For mini open-faced sandwiches, spread mustard on cocktail rye bread. Top with bratwurst slices and onions.   *Makes 30 to 36 appetizers*

Tip: Choose a light-tasting beer for cooking brats. Hearty ales might leave the meat tasting slightly bitter.

1½ pounds bratwurst (about 5 or 6 links)
1 can or bottle (12 ounces) beer (not dark)
1 medium onion, thinly sliced
2 tablespoons packed brown sugar
2 tablespoons red wine or cider vinegar
Spicy brown mustard
Cocktail rye bread

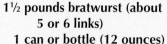

Parmesan Ranch Snack Mix

3 cups bite-size corn
 or rice cereal
2 cups oyster crackers
1 package (5 ounces) bagel
 chips, broken in half
1½ cups pretzel twists
1 cup pistachios
2 tablespoons grated
 Parmesan cheese
¼ cup (½ stick) butter,
 melted
1 package (1 ounce)
 dry ranch salad
 dressing mix
½ teaspoon garlic powder

1. Combine cereal, oyster crackers, bagel chips, pretzels, pistachios and Parmesan cheese in slow cooker; mix gently.

2. Combine butter, salad dressing mix and garlic powder in small bowl. Pour over cereal mixture; toss lightly to coat. Cover; cook on LOW 3 hours.

3. Remove cover; stir gently. Cook, uncovered, 30 minutes.

Makes about 9½ cups snack mix

Starters

Hearty Calico Bean Dip

1. Brown ground beef in large nonstick skillet over medium-high heat, stirring to separate meat. Drain and discard fat. Spoon into slow cooker.

2. Add bacon, beans, onion, brown sugar, ketchup, vinegar and mustard to slow cooker; mix well.

3. Cover; cook on LOW 4 hours or on HIGH 2 hours. Serve with tortilla chips.

Makes 5 to 6 cups dip

¾ **pound ground beef**
½ **pound sliced bacon, crisp-cooked and crumbled**
1 **can (16 ounces) baked beans**
1 **can (15 ounces) Great Northern beans, rinsed and drained**
1 **can (15 ounces) kidney beans, rinsed and drained**
1 **small onion, chopped**
½ **cup brown sugar**
½ **cup ketchup**
1 **tablespoon vinegar**
1 **teaspoon prepared yellow mustard**
Tortilla chips

Beef

Mexican-Style Shredded Beef

1 boneless beef chuck
    shoulder roast (about
    3 pounds)
1 tablespoon ground cumin
1 tablespoon ground
    coriander
1 tablespoon chili powder
1 teaspoon salt
½ teaspoon ground red
    pepper
1 cup salsa or picante
    sauce
2 tablespoons water
1 tablespoon cornstarch

1. Cut roast in half. Combine cumin, coriander, chili powder, salt and red pepper in small bowl. Rub over beef. Place ¼ cup salsa in slow cooker; top with one piece beef. Layer ¼ cup salsa, remaining beef and ½ cup salsa in slow cooker. Cover; cook on LOW 8 to 10 hours or until meat is tender.

2. Remove beef from cooking liquid; cool slightly. Trim and discard excess fat from beef. Shred meat with 2 forks.

3. Let cooking liquid stand 5 minutes to allow fat to rise. Skim off fat. Blend water and cornstarch until smooth; stir into slow cooker. Cook, uncovered, on HIGH 15 minutes or until thickened. Return beef to slow cooker. Cover; cook 15 to 30 minutes or until hot. Adjust seasonings. Serve as meat filling for tacos, fajitas or burritos. Leftover beef may be refrigerated up to 3 days or frozen up to 3 months.
Makes 5 cups filling

Italian Combo Subs

1 tablespoon vegetable oil
1 pound boneless beef round steak, cut into thin strips
1 pound Italian sausage
1 green bell pepper, cut into strips
1 medium onion, thinly sliced
1 can (4 ounces) sliced mushrooms, drained (optional)
Salt and black pepper
1 jar (26 ounces) pasta sauce
2 loaves French bread, cut into 6-inch pieces, split

1. Heat oil in large skillet over medium-high heat. Brown beef in two batches. Place beef in slow cooker.

2. In same skillet, brown sausage, stirring to separate meat. Drain and discard fat. Add sausage to slow cooker.

3. Place bell pepper, onion and mushrooms, if desired, over meat in slow cooker. Season with salt and black pepper. Top with pasta sauce. Cover; cook on LOW 4 to 6 hours. Serve in bread. *Makes 6 servings*

Serving Suggestion: Top with freshly grated Parmesan cheese.

Beef

Easy Family Burritos

1. Place roast in slow cooker; top with salsa. Cover; cook on LOW 8 to 10 hours.

2. Remove beef from slow cooker. Shred meat with 2 forks. Return to slow cooker. Cover; cook 1 to 2 hours.

3. Serve shredded meat wrapped in warm tortillas.   *Makes 8 servings*

Serving Suggestion: Serve burritos with any combination of toppings, such as shredded cheese, sour cream, salsa, lettuce, tomato, onion and guacamole.

Tip: Make a batch of burrito filling and freeze it in family-size portions. It's quick and easy to reheat in the microwave on busy nights when there's no time to cook.

1 boneless beef chuck shoulder roast (2 to 3 pounds)
1 jar (24 ounces) *or* 2 jars (16 ounces each) salsa
Flour tortillas

Beef Bourguignonne

1 to 2 boneless beef top sirloin steaks (about 3 pounds)
½ cup all-purpose flour
4 slices bacon, diced
2 medium carrots, diced
8 small red potatoes, unpeeled, quartered
8 to 10 mushrooms, sliced
20 to 24 pearl onions
3 cloves garlic, minced
1 bay leaf
1 teaspoon dried marjoram
½ teaspoon dried thyme
½ teaspoon salt
Black pepper
2½ cups Burgundy wine or beef broth

1. Cut beef into 1-inch pieces. Coat with flour, shaking off excess; set aside. Cook bacon in large skillet over medium heat until partially cooked. Add beef; brown on all sides. Drain and discard fat.

2. Layer carrots, potatoes, mushrooms, onions, garlic, bay leaf, marjoram, thyme, salt, pepper to taste and beef mixture in slow cooker. Pour wine over all.

3. Cover; cook on LOW 8 to 9 hours or until beef is tender. Remove and discard bay leaf before serving. *Makes 10 to 12 servings*

Hot & Juicy Reuben Sandwiches

1. Trim excess fat from corned beef. Place meat in slow cooker. Add sauerkraut, broth, onion, garlic, caraway seeds and peppercorns.

2. Cover; cook on LOW 7 to 9 hours.

3. Remove beef from slow cooker. Cut across the grain into ¼-inch-thick slices. Divide evenly on 4 slices bread. Top each slice with ½ cup drained sauerkraut mixture and one slice cheese. Spread mustard on remaining 4 bread slices. Close sandwich.

Makes 4 servings

1 mild-cure corned beef
  (about 1½ pounds)
2 cups sauerkraut, drained
½ cup beef broth
1 small onion, sliced
1 clove garlic, minced
¼ teaspoon caraway seeds
4 to 6 peppercorns
8 slices pumpernickel or
  rye bread
4 slices Swiss cheese
  Mustard

Favorite Beef Stew

3 *each* carrots and celery ribs, cut into pieces

2 large potatoes, peeled, cut into ½-inch pieces

1½ cups chopped onions

3 cloves garlic, chopped

4½ teaspoons Worcestershire sauce

¾ teaspoon dried thyme

¾ teaspoon dried basil

½ teaspoon black pepper

1 bay leaf

2 pounds beef stew, cut into 1-inch pieces

1 can (14½ ounces) diced tomatoes, undrained

1 can (14½ ounces) beef broth

½ cup cold water

¼ cup all-purpose flour

1. Layer carrots, celery, potatoes, onions, garlic, Worcestershire sauce, thyme, basil, pepper, bay leaf, beef, tomatoes with juice and broth in slow cooker.

2. Cover; cook on LOW 8 to 9 hours.

3. Remove beef and vegetables to large serving bowl; cover and keep warm. Remove and discard bay leaf. Blend water and flour until smooth. Add ½ cup cooking liquid; mix well. Stir flour mixture into slow cooker. Cook, uncovered, on HIGH 15 minutes or until thickened. Pour sauce over meat and vegetables. Serve immediately.

Makes 6 to 8 servings

Chipotle Taco Filling

1. Brown ground beef in large nonstick skillet over medium-high heat, stirring to separate meat. Drain and discard fat.

2. Place beef, onion, beans, tomatoes with juice, peppers, bouillon, sugar and cumin in slow cooker. Cover; cook on LOW 4 hours or on HIGH 2 hours.

3. Serve filling in taco shells or flour tortillas. Top with shredded lettuce, salsa, shredded cheese and sour cream, if desired. *Makes 8 cups filling*

2 pounds ground beef chuck

2 cups chopped yellow onion

2 cans (15 ounces each) pinto beans, rinsed and drained

1 can (14½ ounces) diced tomatoes with peppers and onions, undrained

2 chipotle peppers in adobo sauce, mashed

1 tablespoon beef bouillon granules

1 tablespoon sugar

1½ teaspoons ground cumin Taco shells

Corned Beef and Cabbage

1 head cabbage
(1½ pounds), cut
into 6 wedges
4 ounces baby carrots
1 corned beef (3 pounds)
with seasoning packet*
1 quart (4 cups) water
⅓ cup prepared mustard
⅓ cup honey

*If seasoning packet is not perforated,
poke several small holes with tip of
paring knife.

1. Place cabbage in slow cooker; top with carrots. Place seasoning packet on top of vegetables. Place corned beef, fat side up, over seasoning packet and vegetables. Add water. Cover; cook on LOW 10 hours.

2. Combine mustard and honey in small bowl.

3. Discard seasoning packet. Slice beef and serve with vegetables and mustard sauce.

Makes 6 servings

Broccoli and Beef Pasta

1. Layer broccoli, onion, basil, oregano, thyme, tomatoes with juice and broth in slow cooker. Cover; cook on LOW 2½ hours.

2. Combine beef and garlic in large nonstick skillet; brown over medium-high heat, stirring to separate meat. Drain and discard fat. Add beef mixture to slow cooker. Cover; cook 2 hours.

3. Stir in tomato paste. Add pasta and cheese. Cover; cook 30 minutes or until cheese melts and mixture is heated through. Sprinkle with additional shredded cheese. *Makes 4 servings*

Serving Suggestion: Serve with garlic bread.

2 cups broccoli florets *or*
   1 package (10 ounces) frozen broccoli, thawed
1 onion, thinly sliced
½ teaspoon dried basil
½ teaspoon dried oregano
½ teaspoon dried thyme
1 can (14½ ounces) Italian-style diced tomatoes, undrained
¾ cup beef broth
1 pound 90% lean ground beef
2 cloves garlic, minced
2 tablespoons tomato paste
2 cups cooked rotini pasta
¾ cup (3 ounces) shredded Cheddar cheese

Italian-Style Pot Roast

2 teaspoons minced garlic
1 teaspoon salt
1 teaspoon dried basil
1 teaspoon dried oregano
¼ teaspoon red pepper
    flakes
1 boneless beef bottom
    round rump or chuck
    shoulder roast (about
    2½ to 3 pounds)
1 large onion, quartered
    and thinly sliced
1½ cups prepared tomato-
    basil or marinara pasta
    sauce
2 cans (15 ounces each)
    Great Northern beans,
    drained
¼ cup shredded fresh basil
    or chopped parsley

1. Combine garlic, salt, basil, oregano and pepper flakes in small bowl; rub over roast. Place half of onion slices into slow cooker. Cut roast in half to fit into slow cooker. Place one half of roast over onion slices; top with remaining onion slices and other half of roast. Pour pasta sauce over roast. Cover; cook on LOW 8 to 9 hours or until roast is fork tender.

2. Remove roast from cooking liquid; tent with foil. Let liquid in slow cooker stand 5 minutes to allow fat to rise. Skim off fat

3. Stir beans into liquid. Cover; cook on HIGH 15 to 30 minutes or until beans are hot. Carve roast across the grain into thin slices. Serve with bean mixture and fresh basil.

Makes 6 to 8 servings

Beef

Best Beef Brisket Sandwich Ever

1. Place brisket, ½ cup cider, garlic, peppercorns, thyme, mustard seed, Cajun seasoning, cumin, celery seed, allspice and cloves in large resealable plastic food storage bag. Seal bag; marinate in refrigerator overnight.

2. Place brisket and marinade in slow cooker. Add remaining 1½ cups cider and beer.

3. Cover; cook on LOW 10 hours or until brisket is tender. Slice brisket and place on sandwich rolls. Strain sauce; drizzle over meat.

Makes 10 to 12 servings

Serving Suggestion: Top with mustard or horseradish sauce.

1 beef brisket (about 3 pounds)
2 cups apple cider, divided
1 head garlic, cloves separated, crushed and peeled
2 tablespoons whole peppercorns
2 tablespoons dried thyme
1 tablespoon mustard seed
1 tablespoon Cajun seasoning
1 teaspoon ground cumin
1 teaspoon celery seed
1 teaspoon ground allspice
2 to 4 whole cloves
1 bottle (12 ounces) dark beer
10 to 12 sourdough sandwich rolls, halved

Slow Cooker Pepper Steak

2 tablespoons vegetable oil
3 pounds boneless beef top sirloin steak, cut into strips
1 tablespoon minced garlic
1 medium onion, chopped
½ cup reduced-sodium soy sauce
2 teaspoons sugar
1 teaspoon salt
½ teaspoon ground ginger
½ teaspoon black pepper
3 green bell peppers, cut into strips
¼ cup cold water
1 tablespoon cornstarch
Hot cooked white rice

1. Heat oil in large skillet over medium-low heat. Brown steak strips in two batches. Add garlic; cook and stir 2 minutes. Transfer steak strips, garlic and pan juices to slow cooker.

2. Add onion, soy sauce, sugar, salt, ginger and black pepper to slow cooker; mix well. Cover; cook on LOW 6 to 8 hours or until meat is tender (up to 10 hours).

3. Add bell pepper strips during final hour of cooking. Blend water and cornstarch until smooth; stir into slow cooker. Cook, uncovered, on HIGH 15 minutes or until thickened. Serve with rice. *Makes 6 to 8 servings*

Suzie's Sloppy Joes

1. Brown ground beef, onion and garlic in large nonstick skillet over medium-high heat in 2 batches, stirring to separate meat. Drain and discard fat.

2. Combine ketchup, bell pepper, Worcestershire sauce, brown sugar, vinegar, mustard and chili powder in slow cooker. Stir in beef mixture.

3. Cover; cook on LOW 6 to 8 hours. Spoon into hamburger buns.

Makes 8 servings

3 pounds 90% lean ground beef
1 cup chopped onion
3 cloves garlic, minced
1¼ cups ketchup
1 cup chopped red bell pepper
5 tablespoons Worcestershire sauce
4 tablespoons brown sugar
3 tablespoons vinegar
3 tablespoons prepared mustard
2 teaspoons chili powder
Hamburger buns

Beef and Vegetables in Rich Burgundy Sauce

1 package (8 ounces) sliced
    mushrooms
1 package (8 ounces) baby
    carrots
1 green bell pepper, cut
    into strips
1 boneless beef chuck roast
    (2½ pounds)
1 can (10½ ounces)
    condensed golden
    mushroom soup
¼ cup dry red wine or beef
    broth
1 tablespoon Worcestershire
    sauce
1 package (1 ounce) dry
    onion soup mix
¼ teaspoon black pepper
3 tablespoons cornstarch
2 tablespoons water
4 cups hot cooked noodles

1. Place mushrooms, carrots and bell pepper in slow cooker. Place roast on top of vegetables. Combine mushroom soup, wine, Worcestershire sauce, soup mix and black pepper in medium bowl; mix well. Pour soup mixture over roast. Cover; cook on LOW 8 to 10 hours.

2. Transfer roast to cutting board; cover with foil. Let stand 10 to 15 minutes before slicing.

3. Blend cornstarch and water until smooth; stir into slow cooker. Cook, uncovered, on HIGH 15 minutes or until thickened. Serve beef and vegetables with sauce over noodles. *Makes 6 to 8 servings*

Barbecued Beef Sandwiches

1. Cut roast in half and place into slow cooker. Combine ketchup, onion, vinegar, molasses, Worcestershire sauce, garlic, salt, mustard, black pepper, garlic powder and pepper flakes in large bowl. Pour barbecue sauce mixture over roast. Cover; cook on LOW 8 to 10 hours.

2. Remove roast from sauce; cool slightly. Trim and discard excess fat from beef. Shred meat with 2 forks. Let sauce stand 5 minutes to allow fat to rise. Skim off fat.

3. Return shredded meat to slow cooker. Stir meat to evenly coat with sauce. Adjust seasonings. Cover; cook 15 to 30 minutes or until hot. Spoon filling into sandwich buns and top with additional sauce. *Makes 12 servings*

3 pounds boneless beef
   chuck shoulder roast
2 cups ketchup
1 medium onion, chopped
¼ cup cider vinegar
¼ cup dark molasses
2 tablespoons
   Worcestershire sauce
2 cloves garlic, minced
½ teaspoon salt
½ teaspoon dry mustard
½ teaspoon black pepper
¼ teaspoon garlic powder
¼ teaspoon red pepper
   flakes
Sesame seed buns, split

Slow-Cooked Korean Beef Short Ribs

4 to 4½ pounds beef short ribs

¼ cup chopped green onions with tops

¼ cup soy or tamari sauce

¼ cup beef broth or water

1 tablespoon brown sugar

2 teaspoons minced fresh ginger

2 teaspoons minced garlic

½ teaspoon black pepper

2 teaspoons dark sesame oil

Hot cooked rice or linguini pasta

2 teaspoons sesame seeds, toasted

1. Place ribs in slow cooker. Combine green onions, soy sauce, broth, brown sugar, ginger, garlic and pepper in medium bowl; mix well and pour over ribs. Cover; cook on LOW 7 to 8 hours or until ribs are fork tender.

2. Remove ribs from cooking liquid; cool slightly. Trim excess fat. Cut rib meat into bite-size pieces, discarding bones and fat. Let cooking liquid stand 5 minutes to allow fat to rise. Skim off fat.

3. Stir sesame oil into liquid. Return beef to slow cooker. Cover; cook 15 to 30 minutes or until hot. Serve with rice; garnish with sesame seeds.

Makes 6 servings

Variation: Three pounds boneless short ribs can be substituted for beef short ribs.

Fiery Chili Beef

1. Cut flank steak into 6 evenly-sized pieces. Combine flank steak, tomatoes with juice, beans, onion, garlic, salt, cumin and black pepper in slow cooker.

2. Dice chile pepper. Add pepper and adobo sauce to slow cooker; mix well.

3. Cover; cook on LOW 7 to 8 hours. Serve with tortillas.   *Makes 6 servings*

Note: Chipotle chile peppers are dried, smoked jalapeño peppers with a very hot yet smoky, sweet flavor. They can be found dried, pickled and canned in adobo sauce.

1 to 2 beef flank steaks
   (1 to 1½ pounds)
1 can (28 ounces) diced
   tomatoes, undrained
1 can (15 ounces) pinto
   beans, rinsed and
   drained
1 medium onion, chopped
2 cloves garlic, minced
½ teaspoon salt
½ teaspoon ground cumin
¼ teaspoon black pepper
1 canned chipotle chile
   pepper in adobo sauce
1 teaspoon adobo sauce
   from canned chile
   pepper
   Flour tortillas

Deviled Beef Short Rib Stew

4 pounds beef short ribs, trimmed

2 pounds small red potatoes, scrubbed and quartered

8 carrots, peeled and cut into chunks

2 onions, cut into thick wedges

1 bottle (12 ounces) beer or non-alcoholic malt beverage

8 tablespoons *French's®* Bold n' Spicy Brown Mustard, divided

3 tablespoons *French's®* Worcestershire Sauce, divided

2 tablespoons cornstarch

1. Broil ribs 6 inches from heat on rack in broiler pan 10 minutes or until well browned, turning once. Place vegetables in bottom of slow cooker. Place ribs on top of vegetables.

2. Combine beer, *6 tablespoons* mustard and *2 tablespoons* Worcestershire in medium bowl. Pour into slow cooker. Cover; cook on high 5 hours* or until meat is tender.

3. Transfer meat and vegetables to platter; keep warm. Strain fat from broth; pour broth into saucepan. Combine cornstarch with *2 tablespoons cold water* in small bowl. Stir into broth with remaining *2 tablespoons* mustard and *1 tablespoon* Worcestershire. Heat to boiling. Reduce heat to medium-low. Cook 1 to 2 minutes or until thickened, stirring often. Serve gravy with meat and vegetables. Serve meat with additional mustard.

Makes 6 servings (with 3 cups gravy)

*Or cook 10 hours on low.

Tip: Prepare ingredients the night before for quick assembly in the morning. Store separately in the refrigerator until ready to use.

Classic Beef & Noodles

1. Heat oil in large skillet. Brown beef on all sides. (Work in batches, if necessary.) Drain and discard fat.

2. Combine beef, mushrooms, onion, garlic, salt, oregano, pepper, marjoram and bay leaf in slow cooker. Pour in beef broth and sherry. Cover; cook on LOW 8 to 10 hours or on HIGH 4 to 5 hours. Remove and discard bay leaf.

3. Combine sour cream, flour and water in small bowl. Stir about 1 cup liquid from slow cooker into sour cream mixture. Stir mixture back into slow cooker. Cook, uncovered, on HIGH 30 minutes or until thickened and bubbly. Serve over noodles.

Makes 8 servings

1 tablespoon vegetable oil
2 pounds beef stew, cut into 1-inch pieces
¼ pound mushrooms, sliced into halves
2 tablespoons chopped onion
2 cloves garlic, minced
1 teaspoon salt
1 teaspoon dried oregano
½ teaspoon black pepper
¼ teaspoon dried marjoram
1 bay leaf
1½ cups beef broth
⅓ cup dry sherry
1 cup (8 ounces) sour cream
½ cup all-purpose flour
¼ cup water
4 cups hot cooked noodles

60 frozen fully-cooked meatballs
3 cups chopped onions
1½ cups water
1 cup red wine
2 packages (about 1 ounce each) beef gravy mix
¼ cup ketchup
1 tablespoon dried oregano
1 package (8 ounces) curly noodles

Meatballs in Burgundy Sauce

1. Combine meatballs, onions, water, wine, gravy mix, ketchup and oregano in slow cooker; stir to blend.

2. Cover; cook on HIGH 5 hours.

3. Meanwhile cook noodles according to package directions. Serve meatballs with noodles. *Makes 6 to 8 servings*

Serving Suggestion: Serve meatballs as an appetizer with remaining sauce as a dip.

Swiss Steak

1. Place onion and garlic in slow cooker.

2. Dredge steak in flour seasoned with salt and pepper. Shake off excess flour. Place steak in slow cooker. Add tomatoes with juice. Cover with tomato soup. Add potatoes, peas and carrots and celery.

3. Cover; cook on LOW 6 to 8 hours or until meat and potatoes are tender.

Makes 8 servings

Variation: Add a package of thawed frozen corn or green beans to this recipe for a very easy, family favorite meal.

1 onion, sliced into thick rings
1 clove garlic, minced
1 boneless beef round steak (about 2 pounds), cut into 8 pieces
All-purpose flour
Salt and black pepper
1 can (28 ounces) whole tomatoes, undrained
1 can (10¾ ounces) condensed tomato soup
3 medium unpeeled potatoes, diced
1 package (16 ounces) frozen peas and carrots
1 cup sliced celery

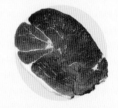

Beef Roll-Ups

1 boneless beef round
    steak (1½ pounds),
    ½ inch thick
4 slices bacon
½ cup diced green bell
    pepper
¼ cup diced onion
¼ cup diced celery
1 can (10 ounces) beef
    gravy

1. Cut steak into 4 pieces. Place 1 bacon slice on each piece.

2. Combine bell pepper, onion and celery in medium bowl. Place about ¼ cup mixture on each piece of meat. Roll up meat; secure with toothpicks.

3. Place beef rolls in slow cooker. Pour gravy evenly over top. Cover; cook on LOW 8 to 10 hours. Skim fat; discard. *Makes 4 servings*

Slow Cooker Steak Fajitas

1. Cut flank steak lengthwise in half, then crosswise into thin strips. Combine beef strips, onion, salsa, lime juice, cilantro, garlic, chili powder, cumin and salt in slow cooker.

2. Cover; cook on LOW 5 to 6 hours. Add bell peppers. Cover; cook 1 hour.

3. Serve with flour tortillas and additional salsa. *Makes 4 servings*

1 beef flank steak (about 1 pound)
1 medium onion, cut into strips
½ cup medium salsa
2 tablespoons fresh lime juice
2 tablespoons chopped fresh cilantro
2 cloves garlic, minced
1 tablespoon chili powder
1 teaspoon ground cumin
½ teaspoon salt
1 small green bell pepper, cut into strips
1 small red bell pepper, cut into strips
Flour tortillas, warmed

Pork & Lamb

Cajun-Style Country Ribs

2 cups baby carrots
1 large onion, coarsely chopped
1 large green bell pepper, cut into 1-inch pieces
1 large red bell pepper, cut into 1-inch pieces
2 teaspoons minced garlic
2 tablespoons Cajun or Creole seasoning, divided
3½ to 4 pounds pork country-style ribs
1 can (14½ ounces) stewed tomatoes, undrained
2 tablespoons water
1 tablespoon cornstarch
Hot cooked rice

1. Combine carrots, onion, bell peppers, garlic and 2 teaspoons Cajun seasoning in slow cooker; mix well.

2. Trim excess fat from ribs. Cut into individual riblets. Sprinkle 1 tablespoon Cajun seasoning over ribs; place in slow cooker over vegetables. Pour tomatoes with juice over ribs (slow cooker will be full). Cover; cook on LOW 6 to 8 hours or until ribs are fork tender.

3. Remove ribs and vegetables from cooking liquid to serving platter. Let liquid stand 5 minutes to allow fat to rise. Skim off fat. Blend water, cornstarch and remaining 1 teaspoon Cajun seasoning until smooth; stir into slow cooker. Cook, uncovered, on HIGH 15 to 30 minutes or until sauce is thickened. Return ribs and vegetables to sauce; carefully stir to coat. Serve with rice.

Makes 6 to 8 servings

Sweet and Sour Spareribs

4 pounds pork spareribs
2 cups dry sherry or
   chicken broth
½ cup pineapple, mango
   or guava juice
⅓ cup chicken broth
2 tablespoons packed light
   brown sugar
2 tablespoons cider vinegar
2 tablespoons soy sauce
1 clove garlic, minced
½ teaspoon salt
¼ teaspoon black pepper
⅛ teaspoon red pepper
   flakes
2 tablespoons cornstarch
¼ cup water

1. Preheat oven to 400°F. Place ribs in foil-lined shallow roasting pan. Bake 30 minutes, turning over after 15 minutes. Remove from oven. Slice meat into 2-rib portions. Place ribs in 5-quart slow cooker. Add sherry, juice, broth, brown sugar, vinegar, soy sauce, garlic, salt, black pepper and pepper flakes to slow cooker.

2. Cover; cook on LOW 6 hours. Transfer ribs to platter; keep warm. Let liquid in slow cooker stand 5 minutes to allow fat to rise. Skim off fat.

3. Blend cornstarch and water until smooth. Whisk in ¼ cup liquid from slow cooker. Stir mixture into liquid in slow cooker. Cook, uncovered, on HIGH 15 minutes or until slightly thickened.　*Makes 4 servings*

Pork & Lamb

Panama Pork Stew

1. Place potatoes, corn, green beans and onion in slow cooker. Top with pork.

2. Combine tomatoes with juice, water, chili powder, salt and coriander in medium bowl. Pour over pork in slow cooker.

3. Cover; cook on LOW 7 to 9 hours.

Makes 6 servings

2 sweet potatoes (about ¾ pound), peeled and cut into 2-inch pieces

1 package (10 ounces) frozen corn

1 package (9 ounces) frozen cut green beans

1 cup chopped onion

1¼ pounds pork stew meat, cut into 1-inch cubes

1 can (14½ ounces) diced tomatoes, undrained

¼ cup water

1 to 2 tablespoons chili powder

½ teaspoon salt

½ teaspoon ground coriander

Italian-Style Sausage with Rice

1 pound mild Italian
  sausage, cut into
  1-inch pieces
2 cans (15 ounces each)
  pinto beans, rinsed and
  drained
1 cup pasta sauce
1 green bell pepper, cut
  into strips
1 small onion, halved and
  sliced
½ teaspoon salt
¼ teaspoon black pepper
  Hot cooked rice
  Chopped fresh basil

1. Brown sausage in large nonstick skillet over medium heat. Drain and discard fat.

2. Place sausage, beans, pasta sauce, bell pepper, onion, salt and black pepper in slow cooker. Cover; cook on LOW 4 to 6 hours.

3. Serve with rice. Garnish with basil.

Makes 4 to 5 servings

Ale'd Pork and Sauerkraut

1. Place sauerkraut in slow cooker. Sprinkle sugar evenly over sauerkraut; pour beer over all. Place pork, fat side up, on top of sauerkraut mixture; sprinkle evenly with salt, garlic powder, pepper and paprika.

2. Cover; cook on HIGH 6 hours.

3. Remove pork to serving platter. Remove sauerkraut with slotted spoon; arrange around pork. Spoon ½ to ¾ cup cooking liquid over sauerkraut, if desired.

Makes 6 to 8 servings

1 jar (32 ounces) sauerkraut, undrained
1½ tablespoons sugar
1 bottle (12 ounces) dark beer or ale
3½ pounds boneless pork shoulder or pork butt roast
½ teaspoon salt
¼ teaspoon garlic powder
¼ teaspoon black pepper
Paprika

1 can (10¾ ounces)
    condensed beef
    consommé
½ cup water
3 tablespoons soy sauce
2 tablespoons honey
2 tablespoons maple syrup
2 tablespoons barbecue
    sauce
½ teaspoon dry mustard
2 pounds pork baby back
    ribs, trimmed

Honey Ribs

1. Combine consommé, water, soy sauce, honey, maple syrup, barbecue sauce and mustard in slow cooker; mix well.

2. Cut ribs into 3- to 4-rib portions. Add ribs to slow cooker. (If ribs are especially fatty, broil 10 minutes before adding to slow cooker.)

3. Cover; cook on LOW 6 to 8 hours or on HIGH 4 to 6 hours or until ribs are tender. Cut into individual ribs. Serve with sauce. *Makes 4 servings*

Pork & Lamb

Spicy Asian Pork Filling

1. Cut roast into 2- to 3-inch chunks. Combine pork, soy sauce, chili garlic sauce and ginger in slow cooker; mix well. Cover; cook on LOW 8 to 10 hours or until pork is fork tender.

2. Remove roast from cooking liquid; cool slightly. Trim and discard excess fat. Shred meat with 2 forks. Let cooking liquid stand 5 minutes to allow fat to rise. Skim off fat.

3. Blend water, cornstarch and sesame oil until smooth; stir into slow cooker. Cook, uncovered, on HIGH until thickened. Add shredded meat to slow cooker; mix well. Cover; cook 15 to 30 minutes or until hot. *Makes 5½ cups filling*

Spicy Asian Pork Bundles: Place ¼ cup pork filling into large lettuce leaves. Wrap to enclose. Makes about 20 bundles.

Moo Shu Pork: Lightly spread plum sauce over warm small flour tortillas. Spoon ¼ cup pork filling and ¼ cup stir-fried vegetables into flour tortillas. Wrap to enclose. Serve immediately. Makes about 20 wraps.

1 boneless pork sirloin roast (about 3 pounds)
½ cup soy or tamari sauce
1 tablespoon garlic chili sauce or chili paste
2 teaspoons minced fresh ginger
2 tablespoons water
1 tablespoon cornstarch
2 teaspoons dark sesame oil

Slow-Cooked Kielbasa in a Bun

1 pound kielbasa links
1 large onion, thinly sliced
1 large green bell pepper,
    cut into strips
¼ teaspoon salt
¼ teaspoon dried thyme
¼ teaspoon black pepper
½ cup chicken broth
4 hoagie rolls, split

1. Brown kielbasa in nonstick skillet over medium-high heat. Place kielbasa in slow cooker. Add onion, bell pepper, salt, thyme and pepper. Stir in broth.

2. Cover; cook on LOW 7 to 8 hours.

3. Place kielbasa in rolls. Top with onion and bell pepper.

Makes 4 servings

Serving Suggestion: For a zesty flavor, top sandwiches with pickled peppers and a dollop of mustard.

Barbara's Pork Chop Dinner

1. Heat butter and oil in large skillet. Brown pork chops on both sides. Set aside.

2. Combine soup, mushrooms, mustard, chicken broth, garlic, salt, basil and pepper in slow cooker. Add potatoes and onion; stir to coat. Place pork chops on top of potato mixture.

3. Cover; cook on LOW 8 to 10 hours or on HIGH 4 to 5 hours. Sprinkle with parsley just before serving.

Makes 6 servings

1 tablespoon butter
1 tablespoon olive oil
6 pork loin chops
1 can (10¾ ounces) condensed cream of chicken soup
1 can (4 ounces) mushrooms, drained and chopped
¼ cup Dijon mustard
¼ cup chicken broth
2 cloves garlic, minced
½ teaspoon salt
½ teaspoon dried basil
¼ teaspoon black pepper
6 red potatoes, unpeeled, cut into thin slices
1 onion, sliced
  Chopped fresh parsley

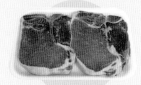

Stew Provençal

2 cans (14½ ounces each) beef broth, divided
⅓ cup all-purpose flour
1 to 2 pork tenderloins (about 2 pounds), trimmed and diced
4 red potatoes, unpeeled, cut into cubes
2 cups frozen cut green beans, thawed
1 onion, chopped
2 cloves garlic, minced
1 teaspoon salt
1 teaspoon dried thyme
½ teaspoon black pepper

1. Blend ¾ cup beef broth and flour until smooth in small bowl. Set aside.

2. Add remaining broth, pork, potatoes, beans, onion, garlic, salt, thyme and pepper to slow cooker; mix well.

3. Cover; cook on LOW 8 to 10 hours or on HIGH 4 to 5 hours. Stir flour mixture into slow cooker. Cook, uncovered, on HIGH 30 minutes or until thickened.

Makes 8 servings

Shredded Pork Wraps

1. Combine ¼ cup salsa and cornstarch in small bowl; stir until smooth. Pour mixture into slow cooker. Top with pork roast. Pour remaining ¾ cup salsa over roast.

2. Cover; cook on LOW 6 to 8 hours. Transfer roast to cutting board; cover with foil and let stand 10 to 15 minutes or until cool enough to handle. Trim and discard fat from pork. Shred meat with 2 forks.

3. Divide shredded meat evenly among tortillas. Spoon about 2 tablespoons salsa mixture on top of meat in each tortilla. Top evenly with broccoli slaw and cheese. Fold bottom edge of tortilla over filling; fold in sides. Roll up completely to enclose filling. Serve remaining salsa mixture as dipping sauce.

Makes 6 servings

1 cup salsa, divided
2 tablespoons cornstarch
1 boneless pork sirloin roast (2 pounds)
6 (8-inch) flour tortillas
3 cups broccoli slaw mix
½ cup shredded Cheddar cheese

Red Beans and Rice with Ham

1. Soak beans overnight; rinse and drain.

2. Place beans in slow cooker. Add sausage, ham, onion and water (2½ cups for LOW; 3 cups for HIGH). Season with Mexican seasoning and red pepper.

3. Cover; cook on LOW 7 to 8 hours or on HIGH 3 to 4 hours or until beans are tender, stirring every 2 hours, if necessary. Serve over rice.

Makes 6 servings

1 package (16 ounces) dried red beans
1 pound beef smoked sausage, sliced
1 ham slice (about 8 ounces), cubed
1 small onion, diced
2½ to 3 cups water
1 teaspoon Mexican (adobo) seasoning with pepper
⅛ teaspoon ground red pepper
Hot cooked rice

Pork Meatballs & Sauerkraut

1. Combine ground pork, bread crumbs, egg, milk, 1 teaspoon caraway seeds, salt, Worcestershire sauce and pepper in large bowl. Shape mixture into 2-inch balls. Brown meatballs in large nonstick skillet over medium-high heat.

2. Combine sauerkraut, onion, bacon and remaining 1 teaspoon caraway seeds in slow cooker. Place meatballs on top of sauerkraut mixture.

3. Cover; cook on LOW 6 to 8 hours. Sprinkle with chopped parsley.

Makes 4 to 6 servings

1¼ **pounds ground pork**
¾ **cup dry bread crumbs**
1 **egg, lightly beaten**
2 **tablespoons milk**
2 **teaspoons caraway seeds, divided**
1 **teaspoon salt**
½ **teaspoon Worcestershire sauce**
¼ **teaspoon black pepper**
1 **jar (32 ounces) sauerkraut, drained, squeezed dry and snipped**
½ **cup chopped onion**
6 **slices bacon, crisp-cooked and crumbled**
Chopped parsley

Pork & Lamb

Sweet & Saucy Ribs

2 pounds pork baby
   back ribs
1 teaspoon black pepper
2½ cups barbecue sauce (not
   mesquite flavored)
1 jar (8 ounces) cherry jam
   or preserves
1 tablespoon Dijon
   mustard
¼ teaspoon salt
   Additional salt and black
   pepper (optional)

1. Trim excess fat from ribs. Rub 1 teaspoon pepper over ribs. Cut ribs into 2-rib portions; place in slow cooker.

2. Combine barbecue sauce, jam, mustard and ¼ teaspoon salt in small bowl; pour over ribs.

3. Cover; cook on LOW 6 to 8 hours or until ribs are tender. Season with additional salt and pepper, if desired. Serve ribs with sauce.

Makes 4 servings

Cantonese Pork

1. Cut tenderloins in half lengthwise, then crosswise into ¼-inch slices. Heat oil in large nonstick skillet over medium-low heat. Brown pork on all sides. Drain and discard fat.

2. Place pork, pineapple with juice, tomato sauce, mushrooms, onion, brown sugar, Worcestershire sauce, salt and vinegar in slow cooker.

3. Cover; cook on LOW 6 to 8 hours or on HIGH 4 hours. Serve over rice.

Makes 8 servings

2 pork tenderloins (about 2 pounds)
1 tablespoon vegetable oil
1 can (8 ounces) pineapple chunks in juice, undrained
1 can (8 ounces) tomato sauce
2 cans (4 ounces each) sliced mushrooms, drained
1 medium onion, thinly sliced
3 tablespoons brown sugar
2 tablespoons Worcestershire sauce
1½ teaspoons salt
1½ teaspoons white vinegar
Hot cooked rice

Easy Homemade Barbecue

Water
1 boneless pork shoulder
   (butt) roast (3 to
   4 pounds)
Salt and black pepper
1 bottle (16 ounces)
   barbecue sauce
Hamburger buns or
   sandwich rolls

1. Cover bottom of slow cooker with water. Place roast in slow cooker; season with salt and pepper.

2. Cover; cook on LOW 8 to 10 hours.

3. Remove roast from slow cooker; let stand 15 minutes. Discard liquid remaining in slow cooker. Shred meat with 2 forks. Return meat to slow cooker. Add barbecue sauce; mix well. Cover; cook on HIGH 30 minutes. Serve barbecue mixture in buns. *Makes 8 to 10 servings*

Pork & Lamb

Shredded Apricot Pork Sandwiches

1. Combine onions, preserves, brown sugar, barbecue sauce, vinegar, Worcestershire sauce and pepper flakes in small bowl. Place pork in slow cooker. Pour apricot mixture over pork. Cover; cook on LOW 8 to 9 hours.

2. Transfer pork to cutting board; cool slightly. Shred meat with 2 forks. Let cooking liquid stand 5 minutes to allow fat to rise. Skim off fat.

3. Blend water, cornstarch, ginger, salt and pepper until smooth; stir into slow cooker. Cook, uncovered, on HIGH 15 to 30 minutes or until thickened. Return shredded pork to slow cooker; mix well. Serve in toasted buns.

Makes 10 to 12 sandwiches

Variation: A 4-pound pork shoulder roast, cut into pieces and trimmed of fat, can be substituted for pork loin roast.

2 medium onions, thinly sliced
1 cup apricot preserves
½ cup packed dark brown sugar
½ cup barbecue sauce
¼ cup cider vinegar
2 tablespoons Worcestershire sauce
½ teaspoon red pepper flakes
1 (4-pound) boneless pork top loin roast, trimmed
¼ cup cold water
2 tablespoons cornstarch
1 tablespoon grated fresh ginger
1 teaspoon salt
1 teaspoon black pepper
10 to 12 sesame or onion rolls, toasted

Barbecued Pulled Pork

1 boneless pork shoulder
   or butt roast (3 to
   4 pounds)
1 teaspoon salt
1 teaspoon ground cumin
1 teaspoon paprika
1 teaspoon black pepper
½ teaspoon ground red
   pepper
1 medium onion, thinly
   sliced
1 medium green bell
   pepper, cut into strips
1 bottle (18 ounces)
   barbecue sauce
½ cup packed light brown
   sugar
   Sandwich rolls

1. Trim excess fat from pork. Combine salt, cumin, paprika, black pepper and red pepper in small bowl; rub over roast.

2. Place onion and bell pepper in slow cooker; add pork. Combine barbecue sauce and brown sugar in medium bowl; pour over meat. Cover; cook on LOW 8 to 10 hours.

3. Transfer roast to cutting board. Trim and discard fat from roast. Shred meat with 2 forks. Serve pork with sauce on sandwich rolls.

Makes 4 to 6 servings

Fiesta Rice and Sausage

1. Heat oil in large nonstick skillet over medium-high heat; brown sausage, stirring to separate meat. Add garlic and cumin; cook 30 seconds. Add onions, bell peppers and jalapeño peppers. Cook and stir until onions are tender, about 10 minutes. Place mixture in slow cooker.

2. Stir in beef broth and rice.

3. Cover; cook on LOW 4 to 6 hours or on HIGH 1 to 2 hours.

Makes 10 to 12 servings

1 teaspoon vegetable oil
2 pounds spicy Italian
  sausage, casing
  removed
2 cloves garlic, minced
2 teaspoons ground cumin
4 onions, chopped
4 green bell peppers,
  chopped
3 jalapeño peppers,*
  seeded and minced
4 cups beef broth
2 packages (6¼ ounces
  each) long grain and
  wild rice mix

Jalapeño peppers can sting and irritate the skin; wear rubber gloves when handling peppers and do not touch eyes. Wash hands after handling.

Lamb in Dill Sauce

2 large boiling potatoes,
   peeled and cut into
   1-inch cubes
½ cup chopped onion
1½ teaspoons salt
½ teaspoon black pepper
½ teaspoon dried dill weed
   or 4 sprigs fresh dill
1 bay leaf
2 pounds lamb stew meat,
   cut into 1-inch cubes
1 cup plus 3 tablespoons
   water, divided
2 tablespoons all-purpose
   flour
1 teaspoon sugar
2 tablespoons lemon juice
   Fresh dill (optional)

1. Layer potatoes, onion, salt, pepper, dill, bay leaf, lamb and 1 cup water in slow cooker.

2. Cover; cook on LOW 6 to 8 hours.

3. Remove lamb and potatoes with slotted spoon; cover and keep warm. Remove and discard bay leaf. Blend remaining 3 tablespoons water and flour until smooth. Add ½ cup cooking liquid and sugar; mix well. Stir into slow cooker. Cook, uncovered, on HIGH 15 minutes. Stir in lemon juice. Return lamb and potatoes to slow cooker. Cover; cook 15 minutes or until heated through. Garnish with fresh dill, if desired.   *Makes 6 servings*

Pork & Lamb

Middle Eastern Lamb and Bean Stew

1. Heat oil in large saucepan over medium-high heat. Add lamb shank and brown on all sides. Transfer lamb to slow cooker. Add broth, garlic and peppercorns. Cover; cook on HIGH 2 hours.

2. Add bacon to same skillet. Cook until crisp. Remove bacon to paper towels; crumble. Add ½ stew meat to skillet; brown on all sides. Transfer meat to slow cooker. Brown remaining ½ stew meat with onion, adding additional oil if needed. Transfer mixture to slow cooker. Add beans, carrots and celery. Cover; cook on LOW 6 hours.

3. Transfer lamb shank to cutting board 30 minutes before serving. Remove meat; return to slow cooker. Discard bone. Let cooking liquid stand 5 minutes to allow fat to rise. Skim off fat. Stir in cornstarch mixture. Cook, uncovered, 30 minutes or until thickened. Season with salt and pepper. Garnish with chopped fresh herbs.

Makes 4 to 6 servings

2 tablespoons olive oil
1 lamb shank
4 cups chicken broth
5 cloves garlic, crushed
8 peppercorns
2 slices bacon, chopped
2 pounds boneless lamb stew meat, dredged in ½ cup flour
½ sweet onion, chopped
2 cans (15 ounces each) cannellini beans, rinsed and drained
2 carrots, sliced
2 to 3 stalks celery, diagonally sliced
¼ cup cornstarch mixed with ¼ cup water

Poultry & Fish

Pineapple Chicken and Sweet Potatoes

⅔ cup plus 3 tablespoons
   flour, divided
1 **teaspoon salt**
1 **teaspoon ground nutmeg**
½ **teaspoon ground**
   cinnamon
⅛ **teaspoon onion powder**
⅛ **teaspoon black pepper**
6 **boneless skinless chicken**
   breasts
3 **sweet potatoes, peeled**
   and sliced
1 **can (10¾ ounces)**
   condensed cream
   of chicken soup
½ **cup pineapple juice**
¼ **pound mushrooms, sliced**
2 **teaspoons packed light**
   brown sugar
½ **teaspoon grated orange**
   peel
   Hot cooked rice

1. Combine ⅔ cup flour, salt, nutmeg, cinnamon, onion powder and black pepper in large bowl. Thoroughly coat chicken with flour mixture. Place sweet potatoes on bottom of slow cooker. Top with chicken.

2. Combine soup, pineapple juice, mushrooms, remaining 3 tablespoons flour, brown sugar and orange peel in medium bowl; stir well. Pour soup mixture over chicken.

3. Cover; cook on LOW 8 to 10 hours or on HIGH 3 to 4 hours. Serve chicken and sauce with rice. *Make 6 servings*

Saucy Tropical Turkey

3 to 4 turkey thighs, skin removed (about 2½ pounds)
2 tablespoons oil
1 small onion, halved and sliced
1 can (20 ounces) pineapple chunks, drained
1 red bell pepper, cubed
⅔ cup apricot preserves
3 tablespoons soy sauce
1 teaspoon grated lemon peel
1 teaspoon ground ginger
¼ cup cold water
2 tablespoons cornstarch
Hot cooked rice

1. Rinse turkey and pat dry. Heat oil in large skillet; brown turkey on all sides. Place onion in slow cooker. Transfer turkey to slow cooker; top with pineapple and bell pepper.

2. Combine preserves, soy sauce, lemon peel and ginger in small bowl; mix well. Spoon over turkey. Cover; cook on LOW 6 to 7 hours.

3. Remove turkey from slow cooker; keep warm. Blend water and cornstarch until smooth; stir into slow cooker. Cook, uncovered, on HIGH 15 minutes or until sauce is slightly thickened. Adjust seasonings. Return turkey to slow cooker; cook until hot. Serve with rice. *Makes 6 servings*

Chicken Sausage Pilaf

1. Heat oil in large nonstick skillet. Brown sausage, stirring to separate meat. Add rice and pasta mix to skillet. Cook 1 minute.

2. Place mixture in slow cooker. Add broth, celery, almonds, salt and pepper to slow cooker; mix well.

3. Cover; cook on LOW 7 to 10 hours or on HIGH 3 to 4 hours or until rice is tender.
Makes 4 servings

1 tablespoon vegetable oil
1 pound chicken or turkey sausage, casing removed
1 cup uncooked rice and pasta mix
4 cups chicken broth
2 ribs celery, diced
¼ cup slivered almonds
Salt and black pepper

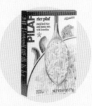

Tuscan Pasta

1 pound boneless skinless chicken breasts, cut into 1-inch pieces

2 cans (14½ ounces each) Italian-style stewed tomatoes

1 can (15 ounces) red kidney beans, rinsed and drained

1 can (15 ounces) tomato sauce

1 cup water

1 jar (4½ ounces) sliced mushrooms, drained

1 medium green bell pepper, chopped

½ cup chopped onion

½ cup chopped celery

4 cloves garlic, minced

1 teaspoon Italian seasoning

6 ounces uncooked thin spaghetti, broken

1. Place chicken, tomatoes, beans, tomato sauce, water, mushrooms, bell pepper, onion, celery, garlic and Italian seasoning in slow cooker.

2. Cover; cook on LOW 4 hours or until vegetables are tender.

3. Stir in spaghetti. Cook on HIGH 10 minutes; stir. Cover; cook 35 minutes or until pasta is tender.

Makes 8 servings

Easy Chicken Alfredo

1. Combine chicken, onion, chives, basil, oil, lemon pepper and ginger in slow cooker; mix well. Add broccoli, bell pepper, water chestnuts, carrots and garlic; mix well.

2. Cover; cook on LOW 8 hours or on HIGH 4 hours.

3. Add Alfredo sauce. Cover; cook on HIGH 30 minutes or until heated through. Serve over noodles.

Makes 6 servings

1½ **pounds boneless skinless chicken breasts, cut into ½-inch pieces**
1 **medium onion, chopped**
1 **tablespoon dried chives**
1 **tablespoon dried basil**
1 **tablespoon olive oil**
1 **teaspoon lemon pepper**
¼ **teaspoon ground ginger**
½ **pound broccoli, coarsely chopped**
1 **red bell pepper, chopped**
1 **can (8 ounces) sliced water chestnuts, drained**
1 **cup baby carrots**
3 **cloves garlic, minced**
1 **jar (16 ounces) Alfredo sauce**
   Hot cooked egg noodles

Turkey Breast with Barley-Cranberry Stuffing

2 cups reduced-sodium chicken broth

1 cup uncooked quick-cooking barley

1/2 cup chopped onion

1/2 cup dried cranberries

2 tablespoons slivered almonds, toasted

1/2 teaspoon rubbed sage

1/2 teaspoon garlic-pepper seasoning

Nonstick cooking spray

1 fresh or thawed frozen bone-in turkey breast half (about 2 pounds), skinned

1/3 cup finely chopped fresh parsley

1. Combine broth, barley, onion, cranberries, almonds, sage and garlic-pepper seasoning in slow cooker.

2. Spray large nonstick skillet with cooking spray. Heat over medium heat until hot. Brown turkey breast on all sides; add to slow cooker. Cover; cook on LOW 4 to 6 hours.

3. Transfer turkey to cutting board; cover with foil. Let stand 10 to 15 minutes before carving. Stir parsley into sauce mixture in slow cooker. Serve sliced turkey with sauce and stuffing. *Makes 6 servings*

Poultry & Fish

French Country Slow Cooker Chicken

1. Place onion, carrots and celery in slow cooker. Arrange chicken over vegetables. Sprinkle with tarragon, thyme, salt and pepper.

2. Pour soup over chicken. Sprinkle with dry soup mix. Cover; cook on HIGH 3 to 4 hours, stirring once during cooking.

3. Twenty minutes before serving, blend wine and cornstarch until smooth; stir into slow cooker. Cook, uncovered, 15 minutes or until thickened. Serve over rice.

Makes 6 to 8 servings

1 medium onion, chopped
4 carrots, sliced
4 ribs celery, sliced
6 to 8 boneless skinless chicken breasts (about 1½ to 2 pounds)
1 teaspoon dried tarragon
1 teaspoon dried thyme
Salt and black pepper
1 can (10¾ ounces) condensed cream of chicken soup
1 envelope (1 ounce) dry onion soup mix
⅓ cup white wine or apple juice
2 tablespoons cornstarch
Hot cooked rice

Cream of Chicken Soup

Mom's Tuna Casserole

2 cans (12 ounces each) tuna, drained and flaked

3 cups diced celery

3 cups crushed potato chips, divided

6 hard-cooked eggs, chopped

1 can (10¾ ounces) condensed cream of mushroom soup

1 can (10¾ ounces) condensed cream of celery soup

1 cup mayonnaise

1 teaspoon dried tarragon

1 teaspoon black pepper

1. Combine tuna, celery, 2½ cups potato chips, eggs, soups, mayonnaise, tarragon and pepper in slow cooker; stir well.

2. Cover; cook on LOW 5 to 8 hours.

3. Sprinkle with remaining ½ cup potato chips.

Makes 8 servings

Forty-Clove Chicken

1. Remove skin from chicken. Sprinkle chicken with salt and pepper. Heat oil in large skillet over medium heat. Add chicken; brown on all sides. Remove to platter.

2. Combine wine, vermouth, parsley, basil, oregano and red pepper flakes in large bowl. Add garlic and celery; coat well. Transfer garlic and celery to slow cooker with slotted spoon. Add chicken to remaining herb mixture; coat well. Place chicken on top of celery in slow cooker. Sprinkle lemon juice and peel over chicken; add remaining herb mixture.

3. Cover; cook on LOW 6 hours. Sprinkle with fresh herbs before serving.

Makes 4 to 6 servings

1 frying chicken
   (3 pounds), cut up
   Salt and black pepper
1 to 2 tablespoons olive oil
¼ cup dry white wine
⅛ cup dry vermouth
2 teaspoons dried parsley
   flakes
2 teaspoons dried basil
1 teaspoon dried oregano
   Pinch red pepper flakes
40 cloves garlic (about
   2 heads*), peeled
4 ribs celery, sliced
   Juice and peel of 1 lemon
   Fresh herbs

*The whole garlic bulb is called a head.

Southwest Turkey Tenderloin Stew

1½ pounds turkey
   tenderloins, cut into
   ¾-inch pieces
1 tablespoon chili powder
1 teaspoon ground cumin
¼ teaspoon salt
1 red bell pepper, cut into
   ¾-inch pieces
1 green bell pepper, cut
   into ¾-inch pieces
¾ cup chopped onion
3 cloves garlic, minced
1 can (15½ ounces) chili
   beans in spicy sauce
1 can (14½ ounces) stewed
   tomatoes, undrained
¾ cup prepared salsa or
   picante sauce

1. Place turkey in slow cooker. Sprinkle chili powder, cumin and salt over turkey; toss to coat.

2. Add bell peppers, onion, garlic, beans, tomatoes and salsa; mix well. Cover; cook on LOW 5 to 6 hours.

3. Adjust seasonings. Ladle into 6 bowls. *Makes 6 servings*

Chicken Enchilada Roll-Ups

1. Cut each chicken breast lengthwise into 2 or 3 strips. Combine ½ cup flour and salt in resealable plastic food storage bag. Add chicken strips and shake to coat with flour mixture. Melt butter in large skillet over medium heat. Brown chicken strips in batches 2 to 3 minutes per side. Place chicken in slow cooker.

2. Add chicken broth to skillet; scrape up any browned bits. Pour broth mixture into slow cooker. Add onion, jalapeño peppers and oregano. Cover; cook on LOW 7 to 8 hours or on HIGH 3 to 4 hours.

3. Blend remaining 2 tablespoons flour and cream until smooth; stir into slow cooker. Cook, uncovered, on HIGH 30 minutes or until thickened. Spoon chicken mixture onto center of flour tortillas. Top with 1 cheese slice. Fold up tortillas and serve.   *Makes 6 servings*

Serving Suggestion: This rich creamy chicken mixture can also be served over cooked rice.

1½ pounds boneless skinless chicken breasts
½ cup plus 2 tablespoons all-purpose flour, divided
½ teaspoon salt
2 tablespoons butter
1 cup chicken broth
1 small onion, diced
¼ to ½ cup canned diced jalapeño peppers
½ teaspoon dried oregano
2 tablespoons heavy cream or milk
6 (7- or 8-inch) flour tortillas
6 thin slices American cheese or American cheese with jalapeño peppers

Coq au Vin

2 cups frozen pearl onions, thawed
4 slices thick-cut bacon, crisp-cooked and crumbled
1 cup sliced button mushrooms
1 clove garlic, minced
1 teaspoon dried thyme
⅛ teaspoon black pepper
6 boneless skinless chicken breasts (about 2 pounds)
½ cup dry red wine
¾ cup reduced-sodium chicken broth
¼ cup tomato paste
3 tablespoons all-purpose flour
Hot cooked egg noodles

1. Layer onions, bacon, mushrooms, garlic, thyme, pepper, chicken, wine and broth in slow cooker.

2. Cover; cook on LOW 6 to 8 hours.

3. Remove chicken and vegetables; cover and keep warm. Ladle ½ cup cooking liquid into small bowl; cool slightly. Blend reserved liquid, tomato paste and flour until smooth; stir into slow cooker. Cook, uncovered, on HIGH 15 minutes or until thickened. Serve over noodles. *Makes 6 servings*

Note: Coq au Vin is a classic French dish that is made with bone-in chicken, salt pork or bacon, brandy, red wine and herbs.

Greek-Style Chicken

1. Remove visible fat from chicken; sprinkle chicken with salt and pepper. Heat oil in large skillet over medium-high heat. Brown chicken on all sides. Place in slow cooker.

2. Add broth, lemon, olives, garlic and oregano to slow cooker.

3. Cover; cook on LOW 5 to 6 hours or until chicken is tender. Serve with orzo.

Makes 4 to 6 servings

6 boneless skinless chicken thighs
½ teaspoon salt
½ teaspoon black pepper
1 tablespoon olive oil
½ cup chicken broth
1 lemon, thinly sliced
¼ cup pitted kalamata olives
1 clove garlic, minced
½ teaspoon dried oregano
Hot cooked orzo or rice

Mu Shu Turkey

1 can (16 ounces) plums, drained and pitted
½ cup orange juice
¼ cup finely chopped onion
1 tablespoon minced fresh ginger
¼ teaspoon ground cinnamon
1 pound boneless turkey breast, cut into thin strips
6 (7-inch) flour tortillas
3 cups coleslaw mix

1. Place plums in blender or food processor. Cover; blend until almost smooth. Combine plums, orange juice, onion, ginger and cinnamon in slow cooker; mix well.

2. Place turkey over plum mixture. Cover; cook on LOW 3 to 4 hours.

3. Remove turkey from slow cooker. Divide evenly among tortillas. Spoon about 2 tablespoons plum sauce over turkey in each tortilla; top with about ½ cup coleslaw mix. Fold bottom edge of tortilla over filling; fold in sides. Roll up to completely enclose filling. Repeat with remaining tortillas. Use remaining plum sauce for dipping. *Makes 6 servings*

Chicken and Stuffing

1. Combine flour, seasoned salt and pepper in large resealable plastic food storage bag. Add chicken; shake to coat with flour mixture.

2. Melt butter in large skillet over medium-low heat. Brown chicken on both sides. Place in slow cooker; pour soup over chicken.

3. Prepare stuffing according to package directions, decreasing liquid by half. Arrange stuffing in slow cooker over chicken. Cover; cook on HIGH 3 to 4 hours.

Makes 4 to 6 servings

½ cup all-purpose flour
¾ teaspoon seasoned salt
¾ teaspoon black pepper
4 to 6 boneless skinless chicken breasts (about 1 to 1½ pounds)
¼ cup (½ stick) butter
2 cans (10¾ ounces each) condensed cream of mushroom soup
1 package (12 ounces) seasoned stuffing mix, plus ingredients to prepare mix

Poultry & Fish

Slow-Simmered Jambalaya

2 cans (14½ ounces each)
    stewed tomatoes,
    undrained
2 cups diced boiled ham
2 medium onions, chopped
1 medium green bell
    pepper, diced
2 ribs celery, sliced
1 cup uncooked long-grain
    rice
2 tablespoons vegetable oil
2 tablespoons ketchup
3 cloves garlic, minced
½ teaspoon dried thyme
½ teaspoon black pepper
⅛ teaspoon ground cloves
1 pound fresh or frozen
    shrimp, peeled and
    deveined

1. Thoroughly mix tomatoes, ham, onions, bell pepper, celery, rice, oil, ketchup, garlic, thyme, black pepper and cloves in slow cooker.

2. Cover; cook on LOW 8 to 10 hours.

3. One hour before serving, increase heat to HIGH. Stir in uncooked shrimp. Cover; cook until shrimp are pink and tender. *Makes 4 to 6 servings*

Poultry & Fish

Chinese Cashew Chicken

1. Combine bean sprouts, chicken, soup, celery, onion, mushrooms, butter and soy sauce in slow cooker; mix well.

2. Cover; cook on LOW 4 to 6 hours or on HIGH 3 to 4 hours.

3. Stir in cashews just before serving. Serve with rice.

Makes 4 servings

1 pound fresh bean sprouts
    or 1 can (16 ounces)
    bean sprouts, drained
2 cups sliced cooked
    chicken
1 can (10¾ ounces)
    condensed cream
    of mushroom soup
1 cup sliced celery
½ cup chopped green
    onions
1 can (4 ounces) sliced
    mushrooms, drained
3 tablespoons butter
1 tablespoon soy sauce
1 cup cashews
    Hot cooked rice

Turkey and Macaroni

1 teaspoon vegetable oil
1½ pounds ground turkey
2 cans (10¾ ounces each) condensed tomato soup, undiluted
2 cups uncooked macaroni, cooked and drained
1 can (16 ounces) corn, drained
½ cup chopped onion
1 can (4 ounces) sliced mushrooms, drained
2 tablespoons ketchup
1 tablespoon mustard
Salt and black pepper

1. Heat oil in large skillet over medium-high heat. Brown turkey, stirring to separate meat. Transfer turkey to slow cooker.

2. Add soup, macaroni, corn, onion, mushrooms, ketchup, mustard, salt and pepper to slow cooker; mix well.

3. Cover; cook on LOW 7 to 9 hours or on HIGH 3 to 4 hours.

Makes 4 to 6 servings

Poultry & Fish

Summer Squash Stew

1. Combine sausage, tomatoes with juice, squash, zucchini, onion, and seasonings in slow cooker; mix well.

2. Cover; cook on LOW 3 hours.

3. Sprinkle cheese over stew. Cook, uncovered, 15 minutes or until cheese melts.

Makes 6 servings

2 pounds cooked Italian turkey sausage or diced cooked chicken

4 cans (14½ ounces each) diced seasoned tomatoes, undrained

5 medium yellow squash, thinly sliced

5 medium zucchini, thinly sliced

1 onion, finely chopped

2 tablespoons dried Italian herb seasoning

1 tablespoon dried tomato, basil and garlic salt-free spice seasoning

4 cups (16 ounces) shredded Mexican cheese blend

Coconut Chicken Curry

1 tablespoon vegetable oil
4 boneless skinless chicken breasts
3 medium potatoes, peeled and chopped
1 medium onion, sliced
1 can (14 ounces) coconut milk
1 cup chicken broth
1½ teaspoons curry powder
1 teaspoon hot pepper sauce
½ teaspoon salt
½ teaspoon black pepper
1 package (10 ounces) frozen peas
Hot cooked rice

1. Heat oil in large skillet over medium-high heat. Brown chicken breasts on both sides. Place potatoes and onion in slow cooker. Top with chicken breasts.

2. Combine coconut milk, broth, curry powder, pepper sauce, salt and pepper in medium bowl. Pour over chicken. Cover; cook on LOW 6 to 8 hours.

3. About 30 minutes before serving, add peas to slow cooker. Serve over rice.

Makes 4 servings

Turkey Mushroom Stew

1. Layer turkey, onions and mushrooms in slow cooker. Cover; cook on LOW 4 hours.

2. Remove turkey and vegetables to serving bowl. Blend flour, half-and-half, salt, tarragon and pepper until smooth; stir into slow cooker. Return cooked vegetables and turkey to slow cooker. Stir in peas. Cover; cook on HIGH 1 hour or until sauce is thickened and peas are heated through.

3. Stir in sour cream just before serving. Serve in puff pastry shells.

Makes 4 servings

1 pound turkey cutlets, cut
   into 4×1-inch strips
1 small onion, thinly sliced
2 tablespoons minced
   green onion with top
½ pound mushrooms, sliced
2 to 3 tablespoons flour
1 cup half-and-half or milk
1 teaspoon salt
1 teaspoon dried tarragon
   Black pepper
½ cup frozen peas
½ cup sour cream
   Puff pastry shells

Slow-Simmered Curried Chicken

1½ cups chopped onions
1 medium green bell pepper, chopped
1 pound boneless skinless chicken breasts or thighs, cut into bite-size pieces
1 cup medium salsa
2 teaspoons grated fresh ginger
½ teaspoon garlic powder
½ teaspoon red pepper flakes
¼ cup chopped fresh cilantro
1 teaspoon sugar
1 teaspoon curry powder
¾ teaspoon salt
Hot cooked rice

1. Place onions and bell pepper in slow cooker. Top with chicken. Combine salsa, ginger, garlic powder and pepper flakes in small bowl; spoon over chicken.

2. Cover; cook on LOW 5 to 6 hours or until chicken is tender.

3. Combine cilantro, sugar, curry powder and salt in small bowl; stir into slow cooker. Cover; cook on HIGH 15 minutes or until hot. Serve with rice.

Makes 4 servings

Thai Turkey & Noodles

1. Place turkey, bell pepper, 1 cup broth, soy sauce, garlic, pepper flakes and salt in slow cooker. Cover; cook on LOW 3 to 4 hours.

2. Blend cornstarch and remaining ¼ cup broth until smooth. Stir green onions, peanut butter and cornstarch mixture into slow cooker. Cook, uncovered, on HIGH 30 minutes or until thickened. Stir well.

3. Serve over vermicelli. Sprinkle with peanuts and cilantro.

Makes 6 servings

Variation: Substitute ramen noodles for the vermicelli. Discard the flavor packet from ramen soup mix and drop the noodles into boiling water. Cook the noodles 2 to 3 minutes or until just tender. Drain and serve hot.

1½ pounds turkey tenderloins, cut into ¾-inch pieces
1 red bell pepper, cut into short, thin strips
1¼ cups reduced-sodium chicken broth, divided
¼ cup soy sauce
3 cloves garlic, minced
¾ teaspoon red pepper flakes
¼ teaspoon salt
2 tablespoons cornstarch
3 green onions, sliced
⅓ cup peanut butter
12 ounces hot cooked vermicelli pasta
¾ cup peanuts or cashews, chopped
¾ cup chopped cilantro

2 medium green bell
    peppers, cut into
    thin strips
1 large onion, quartered
    and thinly sliced
4 chicken thighs
4 chicken drumsticks
1 tablespoon chili powder
2 teaspoons dried oregano
1 jar (16 ounces) chipotle
    salsa
½ cup ketchup
2 teaspoons ground cumin
½ teaspoon salt
    Hot cooked noodles

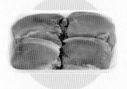

Mexicali Chicken

1. Place bell peppers and onion in slow cooker; top with chicken. Sprinkle chili powder and oregano evenly over chicken. Add salsa. Cover; cook on LOW 7 to 8 hours or on HIGH 2 to 3 hours.

2. Remove chicken pieces to serving bowl; keep warm. Stir ketchup, cumin and salt into liquid in slow cooker. Cook, uncovered, on HIGH 15 minutes or until hot.

3. Pour mixture over chicken. Serve with noodles. *Makes 4 servings*

Tip: For thicker sauce, blend 1 tablespoon cornstarch and 2 tablespoons water until smooth. Stir into cooking liquid with ketchup, cumin and salt.

Poultry & Fish

Chili Turkey Loaf

1. Make foil handles for loaf using technique described below. Mix turkey, onion, bread crumbs, chili sauce, eggs, mustard, garlic, salt, Italian seasoning and black pepper in large bowl. Shape into round loaf and place on foil strips. Transfer to bottom of slow cooker using foil handles.

2. Cover; cook on LOW 4½ to 5 hours.

3. Remove loaf from slow cooker using foil handles. Let stand 5 minutes before serving. Cut into wedges and top with salsa.   *Makes 8 servings*

Foil Handles: Tear off three 18×2-inch strips of heavy foil or use regular foil folded to double thickness. Crisscross foil strips in spoke design and place in slow cooker to allow for easy removal of turkey loaf.

2 pounds ground turkey
1 cup chopped onion
⅔ cup Italian seasoned dry bread crumbs
½ cup chopped green bell pepper
½ cup chili sauce
2 eggs, lightly beaten
2 tablespoons horseradish mustard
4 cloves garlic, minced
1 teaspoon salt
½ teaspoon dried Italian seasoning
¼ teaspoon black pepper
Prepared salsa

Sweet Chicken Curry

1 pound boneless skinless chicken breasts, cut into 1-inch pieces
1 large green or red bell pepper, cut into 1-inch pieces
1 large onion, sliced
1 large tomato, seeded and chopped
½ cup prepared mango chutney
¼ cup water
2 tablespoons cornstarch
1½ teaspoons curry powder
Hot cooked rice

1. Place chicken, bell pepper and onion in slow cooker. Top with tomato.

2. Mix chutney, water, cornstarch and curry powder in small bowl. Pour into slow cooker.

3. Cover; cook on LOW 3½ to 4½ hours. Serve over rice. *Makes 4 servings*

South-of-the-Border Cumin Chicken

1. Place bell pepper mixture in slow cooker; arrange chicken on top of peppers.

2. Combine tomatoes, pepper sauce, sugar, 1 teaspoon cumin, salt and oregano in large bowl. Pour over chicken mixture. Cover; cook on LOW 8 hours or on HIGH 4 hours or until meat is just beginning to fall off bone.

3. Place chicken in shallow serving bowl. Stir remaining ¾ teaspoon cumin into tomato mixture and pour over chicken. Sprinkle with cilantro and serve with lime wedges. Serve over cooked rice or with toasted corn tortillas, if desired.

Makes 4 servings

1 package (16 ounces) frozen bell pepper stir-fry mixture *or* 3 bell peppers, thinly sliced*
4 chicken drumsticks
4 chicken thighs
1 can (14½ ounces) stewed tomatoes
1 tablespoon mild pepper sauce
2 teaspoons sugar
1¾ teaspoons ground cumin, divided
1¼ teaspoons salt
1 teaspoon dried oregano
¼ cup chopped cilantro
1 to 2 medium limes, cut into wedges

If using fresh bell peppers, add ½ cup chopped onion.

Herbed Turkey Breast with Orange Sauce

1 large onion, chopped
3 cloves garlic, minced
1 teaspoon dried rosemary
½ teaspoon black pepper
1 boneless skinless turkey
    breast (2 to 3 pounds)
1½ cups orange juice

1. Place onion in slow cooker. Combine garlic, rosemary and pepper in small bowl; set aside. Cut slices about three-fourths of the way through turkey at 2-inch intervals. Rub garlic mixture between slices.

2. Place turkey, cut side up, in slow cooker. Pour orange juice over turkey. Cover; cook on LOW 7 to 8 hours.

3. Serve sauce from slow cooker with sliced turkey.

Makes 4 to 6 servings

Heidi's Chicken Supreme

1. Spray slow cooker with nonstick cooking spray. Combine soup and soup mix in medium bowl; mix well. Layer chicken breasts and soup mixture in slow cooker. Sprinkle with bacon.

2. Cover; cook on HIGH 4 hours or on LOW 8 hours.

3. Stir in sour cream during last hour of cooking.   *Makes 6 servings*

Variation: Condensed cream of mushroom soup or condensed cream of celery soup can be substituted for cream of chicken soup.

1 can (10¾ ounces)
   condensed cream
   of chicken soup
1 package (1 ounce) dry
   onion soup mix
6 boneless skinless chicken
   breasts (about
   1½ pounds)
½ pound bacon, crisp-
   cooked and crumbled
1 container (16 ounces)
   reduced-fat sour cream

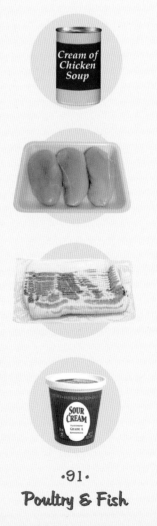

Chilis & Soups

Pasta Fagioli Soup

2 cans (14½ ounces each) reduced-sodium beef broth

1 can (15 ounces) Great Northern beans, rinsed and drained

1 can (14½ ounces) diced tomatoes, undrained

2 medium zucchini, quartered lengthwise and sliced

1 tablespoon olive oil

1½ teaspoons minced garlic

½ teaspoon dried basil

½ teaspoon dried oregano

½ cup uncooked tubetti or small shell pasta

½ cup garlic seasoned croutons

½ cup grated Asiago or Romano cheese

1. Combine broth, beans, tomatoes with juice, zucchini, oil, garlic, basil and oregano in slow cooker; mix well. Cover; cook on LOW 3 to 4 hours.

2. Stir in pasta. Cover; cook 1 hour or until pasta is tender.

3. Serve soup with croutons and cheese. Garnish with fresh basil, if desired.

Makes 5 to 6 servings

Kick'n Chili

2 pounds ground beef
1 tablespoon *each* salt, ground cumin, chili powder, red pepper flakes, paprika, oregano and black pepper
2 cloves garlic, minced
¼ teaspoon ground red pepper
1 tablespoon oil
3 cans (10½ ounces each) diced tomatoes with green chilis
1 jar (16 ounces) salsa
1 onion, chopped

1. Combine ground beef, salt, cumin, chili powder, red pepper flakes, paprika, oregano, black pepper and garlic in large bowl.

2. Heat oil in large skillet over medium-high heat. Brown ground beef mixture, stirring to separate meat. Drain and discard fat. Add tomatoes, salsa and onion; mix well.

3. Transfer to mixture slow cooker. Cover; cook on LOW 4 hours.

Makes 6 servings

Farmhouse Ham and Vegetable Chowder

1. Combine soup, ham, corn, potato, bell pepper and thyme in slow cooker; mix well.

2. Cover; cook on LOW 6 to 8 hours or on HIGH 3 to 4 hours.

3. Stir in broccoli and milk. Cover; cook on HIGH 15 minutes or until broccoli is crisp-tender.

Makes 6 servings

2 cans (10¾ ounces each) condensed cream of celery soup
2 cups diced cooked ham
1 package (10 ounces) frozen corn, thawed
1 large baking potato, cut into ½-inch pieces
1 medium red bell pepper, diced
½ teaspoon dried thyme
2 cups small broccoli florets
½ cup milk

Chicken and Vegetable Chowder

1 pound boneless skinless chicken breasts, cut into 1-inch pieces

1 can (14½ ounces) reduced-sodium chicken broth

1 can (10¾ ounces) condensed cream of potato soup

1 package (10 ounces) frozen broccoli cuts

1 cup sliced carrots

1 jar (4½ ounces) sliced mushrooms, drained

½ cup chopped onion

½ cup whole kernel corn

2 cloves garlic, minced

½ teaspoon dried thyme

⅓ cup half-and-half

1. Combine chicken, broth, soup, broccoli, carrots, mushrooms, onion, corn, garlic and thyme in slow cooker; mix well.

2. Cover; cook on LOW 5 to 6 hours.

3. Stir in half-and-half. Cover; cook on HIGH 15 minutes or until heated through.

Makes 6 servings

Variation: Add ½ cup (2 ounces) shredded Swiss or Cheddar cheese just before serving, stirring over LOW heat until melted.

Chilis & Soups

Hearty Chili Mac

1. Brown ground beef in large nonstick skillet over medium-high heat, stirring to separate meat. Drain and discard fat. Transfer meat to slow cooker. Add tomatoes, onion, garlic, chili powder, salt, cumin, oregano, pepper flakes and black pepper to slow cooker; mix well.

2. Cover; cook on LOW 4 hours.

3. Stir in macaroni. Cover; cook 1 hour.

Makes 4 servings

1 pound 90% lean ground beef
1 can (14½ ounces) diced tomatoes, drained
1 cup chopped onion
1 clove garlic, minced
1 tablespoon chili powder
½ teaspoon salt
½ teaspoon ground cumin
½ teaspoon dried oregano
¼ teaspoon red pepper flakes
¼ teaspoon black pepper
2 cups cooked macaroni

No-Chop Black Bean Soup

3 cans (15 ounces each) black beans, rinsed and drained

1 package (12 ounces) frozen diced green bell peppers

2 cups frozen chopped onion

2 cans (14½ ounces each) chicken broth

1 can (14½ ounces) diced tomatoes with pepper, celery and onion, undrained

1 teaspoon bottled minced garlic

1½ teaspoons ground cumin, divided

2 tablespoons olive oil

¾ teaspoon salt

1. Combine beans, bell peppers, onion, broth, tomatoes with juice, garlic and 1 teaspoon cumin in slow cooker.

2. Cover; cook on LOW 8 to 10 hours or on HIGH 5 hours.

3. Stir in oil, salt and remaining ½ teaspoon cumin just before serving.

Makes 8 servings

Chicken and Wild Rice Soup

1. Combine broth, chicken, water, celery, carrots, rice and seasoning packet, onion and pepper in slow cooker; mix well.

2. Cover; cook on LOW 6 to 7 hours or on HIGH 4 to 5 hours or until chicken is tender.

3. Stir in vinegar. Garnish with parsley.

Makes 9 (1½-cup) servings

3 cans (14½ ounces each) chicken broth
1 pound boneless skinless chicken breasts or thighs, cut into bite-size pieces
2 cups water
1 cup sliced celery
1 cup diced carrots
1 package (6 ounces) converted long grain and wild rice mix with seasoning packet (not quick-cooking or instant rice)
½ cup chopped onion
½ teaspoon black pepper
2 teaspoons white vinegar
1 tablespoon dried parsley flakes

Beef Fajita Soup

1 pound beef stew
1 can (15 ounces) pinto beans, rinsed and drained
1 can (15 ounces) black beans, rinsed and drained
1 can (14½ ounces) diced tomatoes with roasted garlic, undrained
1 can (14½ ounces) beef broth
1 small green bell pepper, thinly sliced
1 small red bell pepper, thinly sliced
1 small onion, thinly sliced
1½ cups water
2 teaspoons ground cumin
1 teaspoon seasoned salt
1 teaspoon black pepper

1. Combine beef, beans, tomatoes with juice, broth, bell peppers, onion, water, cumin, salt and black pepper in slow cooker.

2. Cover; cook on LOW 8 hours.

3. Serve with desired toppings.

Makes 8 servings

Toppings: Serve topped with sour cream, shredded Monterey Jack or Cheddar cheese and chopped olives.

Three-Bean Mole Chili

1. Combine beans, tomatoes with juice, bell pepper, onion, broth, mole paste, cumin, chili powder, coriander and garlic in slow cooker; mix well.

2. Cover; cook on LOW 5 to 6 hours or until vegetables are tender.

3. Serve with desired toppings.

Makes 4 to 6 servings

Serving Suggestion: Serve with a variety of toppings such as sour cream, sliced black olives, shredded lettuce, shredded cheese and chopped tomatoes.

1 (15-ounce) can *each* pinto and black beans, rinsed and drained

1 can (15½ ounces) chili beans in spicy sauce, undrained

1 can (14½ ounces) diced tomatoes with green chilis or chili-style diced tomatoes, undrained

1 large green bell pepper, diced

1 small onion, diced

½ cup beef, chicken or vegetable broth

¼ cup prepared mole paste*

2 teaspoons ground cumin

2 teaspoons chili powder

2 teaspoons ground coriander

2 teaspoons minced garlic

Mole paste is available in the Mexican section of large supermarkets or in specialty markets.

Chilis & Soups

Potato-Crab Chowder

1 package (10 ounces)
frozen corn, thawed
1 cup frozen hash brown
potatoes, thawed
¾ cup finely chopped
carrots
1 teaspoon dried thyme
¾ teaspoon garlic-pepper
seasoning
3 cups chicken broth
½ cup water
1 cup evaporated milk
3 tablespoons cornstarch
1 can (6 ounces) crabmeat,
drained
½ cup sliced green onions

1. Place corn, potatoes and carrots in slow cooker. Sprinkle with thyme and garlic-pepper seasoning. Add broth and water.

2. Cover; cook on LOW 3½ to 4½ hours.

3. Blend evaporated milk and cornstarch until smooth. Stir into slow cooker. Cover; cook on HIGH 1 hour. Just before serving, stir in crabmeat and green onions.

Makes 5 servings

Navy Bean Bacon Chowder

1. Soak beans overnight in cold water.

2. Cook bacon in medium skillet over medium heat. Drain fat; crumble bacon. Drain beans. Combine beans, bacon, carrot, celery, onion, turnip, Italian seasoning and pepper in slow cooker. Add broth. Cover; cook on LOW 8 to 9 hours or until beans are tender.

3. Ladle 2 cups of soup mixture into food processor or blender. Process until smooth; return to slow cooker. Add milk. Cover; cook on HIGH 10 minutes or until heated through.

Makes 6 servings

1½ cups dried navy beans, rinsed
2 cups cold water
6 slices thick-cut bacon
1 medium carrot, diced
1 rib celery, chopped
1 medium onion, chopped
1 small turnip, cut into 1-inch pieces
1 teaspoon dried Italian seasoning
⅛ teaspoon black pepper
1 large can (46 ounces) reduced-sodium chicken broth
1 cup milk

Classic French Onion Soup

¼ cup (½ stick) butter
3 large yellow onions, sliced
1 cup dry white wine
3 cans (14½ ounces each) beef or chicken broth
1 teaspoon Worcestershire sauce
½ teaspoon salt
½ teaspoon dried thyme
4 slices French bread, toasted
1 cup (4 ounces) shredded Swiss cheese

1. Melt butter in large skillet over high heat. Add onions; cook and stir 15 minutes or until onions are soft and lightly browned. Stir in wine.

2. Combine onion mixture, broth, Worcestershire sauce, salt and thyme in slow cooker. Cover; cook on LOW 4 to 4½ hours.

3. Ladle soup into 4 bowls; top with bread slice and cheese.

Makes 4 servings

Chilis & Soups

Simmering Hot & Sour Soup

1. Combine broth, chicken, mushrooms, bamboo shoots, vinegar, soy sauce and chili sauce in slow cooker. Cover; cook on LOW 3 to 4 hours.

2. Stir in tofu and sesame oil. Blend cornstarch and water until smooth. Stir into slow cooker. Cover; cook on HIGH 15 minutes or until soup is thickened.

3. Serve hot; garnish with cilantro.

Makes 4 servings

2 cans (14½ ounces each) chicken broth
1 cup chopped cooked chicken or pork
4 ounces fresh shiitake mushroom caps, sliced
½ cup sliced bamboo shoots, cut into strips
3 tablespoons rice vinegar
2 tablespoons soy sauce
1½ teaspoons Chinese garlic chili sauce
4 ounces firm tofu, well drained and cut into ½-inch pieces
2 teaspoons dark sesame oil
2 tablespoons cornstarch
2 tablespoons cold water
Chopped cilantro

Chilis & Soups

Peppery Potato Soup

2 cans (14½ ounces each) chicken broth
4 small baking potatoes, halved and sliced
1 large onion, quartered and sliced
1 rib celery with leaves, sliced
¼ cup all-purpose flour
¾ teaspoon black pepper
½ teaspoon salt
1 cup half-and-half
1 tablespoon butter
Celery leaves

1. Combine broth, potatoes, onion, celery, flour, pepper and salt in slow cooker; mix well. Cover; cook on LOW 6 to 7½ hours.

2. Stir in half-and-half. Cover; cook 1 hour.

3. Remove slow cooker lid. Slightly crush potato mixture with potato masher. Cook, uncovered, 30 minutes or until slightly thickened. Just before serving, stir in butter. Garnish with celery leaves.

Makes 6 (1¼-cup) servings

Chili with Chocolate

1. Brown ground beef, onion and 1 clove garlic in large nonstick skillet over medium-low heat, stirring to separate meat. Drain and discard fat.

2. Place meat mixture in slow cooker. Add tomatoes with juice, beans with sauce, chili powder, remaining 2 cloves garlic and chocolate; mix well.

3. Cover; cook on LOW 5 to 6 hours. Add cumin, salt, pepper and hot sauce during the last hour of cooking.

Makes 4 servings

1 pound 90% lean ground beef
1 medium onion, chopped
3 cloves garlic, minced and divided
2 cans (14½ ounces each) diced tomatoes, undrained
1 can (15½ ounces) chili beans in mild or spicy sauce, undrained
1 tablespoon chili powder
1 tablespoon grated semisweet baking chocolate
1½ teaspoons ground cumin
½ teaspoon salt
½ teaspoon black pepper
½ teaspoon hot pepper sauce

Vegetable Medley Soup

3 cans (14½ ounces each)
   chicken broth
3 sweet potatoes, peeled
   and chopped
3 zucchini, chopped
2 cups chopped broccoli
2 white potatoes, peeled
   and shredded
1 onion, chopped
1 rib celery, finely chopped
¼ cup (½ stick) butter,
   melted
1 teaspoon black pepper
2 cups half-and-half
   or milk
1 tablespoon salt
1 teaspoon ground cumin

1. Combine broth, sweet potatoes, zucchini, broccoli, white potatoes, onion, celery, butter and pepper; mix well. Pour mixture into slow cooker.

2. Cover; cook on LOW 8 to 10 hours or on HIGH 4 to 5 hours.

3. Add half-and-half, salt and cumin. Cover; cook 30 minutes to 1 hour or until heated through. *Makes 12 servings*

Hamburger Soup

1. Brown ground beef in large nonstick skillet over medium-high heat, stirring to separate meat. Drain and discard fat. Place beef, soup mix, salad dressing mix, seasoned salt and pepper in slow cooker. Add water, tomatoes with juice, tomato sauce and soy sauce; mix well. Add celery and carrots.

2. Cover; cook on LOW 6 to 8 hours.

3. Stir in macaroni and Parmesan cheese. Cover; cook on HIGH 10 to 30 minutes or until heated through.

Makes 6 to 8 servings

1 pound 90% lean ground beef
1 package (1 ounce) dry onion soup mix
1 package (1 ounce) Italian salad dressing mix
¼ teaspoon seasoned salt
¼ teaspoon black pepper
3 cups boiling water
1 can (14½ ounces) diced tomatoes, undrained
1 can (8 ounces) tomato sauce
1 tablespoon soy sauce
1 cup sliced celery
1 cup thinly sliced carrots
2 cups cooked macaroni
¼ cup grated Parmesan cheese

Chilis & Soups

Savory Pea Soup with Sausage

8 ounces smoked sausage, cut lengthwise into halves, then cut into ½-inch pieces

1 package (16 ounces) dried split peas, sorted and rinsed

3 medium carrots, sliced

2 ribs celery, sliced

1 medium onion, chopped

¾ teaspoon dried marjoram

1 bay leaf

2 cans (14½ ounces each) chicken broth

1. Heat medium nonstick skillet over medium heat. Add sausage; cook 5 to 8 minutes or until browned. Drain and discard fat.

2. Transfer sausage to slow cooker. Add peas, carrots, celery, onion, marjoram and bay leaf. Pour broth over mixture.

3. Cover; cook on LOW 4 to 5 hours or until peas are tender. Turn off heat. Remove and discard bay leaf. Cover; let stand 15 minutes to thicken.

Makes 6 servings

Chilis & Soups

Easy Slow-Cooked Chili

1. Cook ground beef, chili powder and cumin in large nonstick skillet over medium heat until browned, stirring frequently; drain. Transfer to slow cooker.

2. Stir in tomatoes with juice, beans, water, ½ *cup* French Fried Onions and *Frank's RedHot* Sauce.

3. Cover; cook on LOW setting for 6 hours or on HIGH for 3 hours. Serve chili topped with sour cream, cheese and remaining onions. *Makes 8 servings*

Variation: For added Cheddar flavor, substitute **French's®** **Cheddar French Fried Onions** for the original flavor.

2 pounds lean ground beef
2 tablespoons chili powder
1 tablespoon ground cumin
1 can (28 ounces) crushed tomatoes in purée, undrained
1 can (15 ounces) red kidney beans, drained and rinsed
1 cup water
2 cups *French's®* French Fried Onions, divided
¼ cup *Frank's® RedHot®* Original Cayenne Pepper Sauce
Sour cream and shredded Cheddar cheese

Chilis & Soups

Creamy Turkey Soup

2 cans (10¾ ounces each) condensed cream of chicken soup

2 cups chopped cooked turkey breast

1 package (8 ounces) sliced mushrooms

1 onion, chopped

1 teaspoon rubbed sage *or* ½ teaspoon dried poultry seasoning

1 cup frozen peas, thawed

½ cup milk

1 jar (about 4 ounces) diced pimiento

1. Combine soup, turkey, mushrooms, onion and sage in slow cooker.

2. Cover; cook on LOW 8 hours or on HIGH 4 hours.

3. Stir in peas, milk and pimiento. Cover; cook on HIGH 15 minutes or until heated through.

Makes 5 to 6 servings

Smoked Sausage Gumbo

1. Combine tomatoes with juice and broth in slow cooker. Sprinkle flour evenly over bottom of small skillet. Cook over high heat without stirring 3 to 4 minutes or until flour begins to brown. Reduce heat to medium; stir flour about 4 minutes. Stir in oil until smooth. Carefully whisk flour mixture into slow cooker.

2. Add sausage, onion, bell pepper, celery, carrot, oregano, thyme and red pepper to slow cooker. Stir well. Cover; cook on LOW 4½ to 5 hours.

3. Serve gumbo over rice. Sprinkle with parsley.   *Makes 4 servings*

Tip: If gumbo thickens upon standing, stir in additional broth.

1 can (14½ ounces) diced tomatoes, undrained
1 cup chicken broth
¼ cup all-purpose flour
2 tablespoons olive oil
¾ pound Polish sausage, cut into ½-inch pieces
1 medium onion, diced
1 green bell pepper, diced
2 ribs celery, chopped
1 carrot, peeled and chopped
2 teaspoons dried oregano
2 teaspoons dried thyme
⅛ teaspoon ground red pepper
Hot cooked rice
Chopped parsley

Italian Beef and Barley Soup

1 boneless beef top
   sirloin steak (about
   1½ pounds)
1 tablespoon vegetable oil
4 medium carrots or
   parsnips, sliced ¼-inch
   thick
1 cup chopped onion
1 teaspoon dried thyme
½ teaspoon dried rosemary
¼ teaspoon black pepper
⅓ cup pearl barley
2 cans (14½ ounces each)
   beef broth
1 can (14½ ounces) diced
   tomatoes with Italian
   seasoning, undrained

1. Cut beef into 1-inch pieces. Heat oil over medium-high heat in large skillet. Brown beef on all sides; set aside.

2. Place carrots and onion in slow cooker; sprinkle with thyme, rosemary and pepper. Top with barley and meat. Pour broth and tomatoes with juice over meat.

3. Cover; cook on LOW 8 to 10 hours.

Makes 6 servings

Chilis & Soups

Campfire Sausage and Potato Soup

1. Cut sausage lengthwise in half, then crosswise into ½-inch pieces. Combine sausage, beans, tomatoes with juice, broth, potato, onion, bell pepper, oregano and sugar in slow cooker.

2. Cover; cook on LOW 8 hours or on HIGH 4 hours.

3. Season with cumin before serving.

Makes 6 to 7 servings

8 ounces kielbasa sausage
1 can (15½ ounces) dark kidney beans, rinsed and drained
1 can (14½ ounces) diced tomatoes, undrained
1 can (10½ ounces) condensed beef broth
1 large baking potato, cut into ½-inch cubes
1 medium onion, diced
1 medium green bell pepper, diced
1 teaspoon dried oregano
½ teaspoon sugar
1 to 2 teaspoons ground cumin

Chilis & Soups

Butternut Squash-Apple Soup

3 packages (12 ounces each) frozen cooked winter squash, thawed and drained

2 cans (14½ ounces each) chicken broth

1 Golden Delicious apple, peeled, cored and chopped

2 tablespoons minced onion

1 tablespoon packed light brown sugar

½ teaspoon ground sage

¼ teaspoon ground ginger

½ cup heavy cream or half-and-half

1. Combine squash, broth, apple, onion, brown sugar, sage and ginger in slow cooker.

2. Cover; cook on LOW about 6 hours or on HIGH about 3 hours.

3. Purée soup in blender, food processor or with electric mixer. Stir in cream just before serving. *Makes 6 to 8 servings*

Tip: For thicker soup, use only 3 cups chicken broth.

1-2-3 Chili

1. Brown ground beef in large nonstick skillet over medium-high heat, stirring to separate meat. Drain and discard fat. Combine beef, tomato sauce and beans with sauce in slow cooker; mix well.

2. Cover; cook on LOW 6 to 8 hours.

3. Serve with cheese and green onions.

Makes 8 servings

2 pounds ground beef
4 cans (8 ounces each)
   tomato sauce
3 cans (15½ ounces each)
   chili beans in mild or
   spicy sauce, undrained
Shredded Cheddar
   cheese
Green onions, sliced

Fiesta Black Bean Soup

6 cups chicken broth

¾ pound potatoes, peeled and diced

1 can (15 ounces) black beans, rinsed and drained

½ pound ham, diced

½ onion, diced

1 can (4 ounces) chopped jalapeño peppers

2 cloves garlic, minced

2 teaspoons dried oregano

1½ teaspoons dried thyme

1 teaspoon ground cumin

Toppings: sour cream, chopped bell pepper and chopped tomatoes

1. Combine broth, potatoes, beans, ham, onion, jalapeños, garlic, oregano, thyme and cumin in slow cooker; mix well.

2. Cover; cook on LOW 8 to 10 hours or on HIGH 4 to 5 hours.

3. Adjust seasonings. Serve with desired toppings.

Makes 6 to 8 servings

Chilis & Soups

Red Bean Soup with Andouille Sausage

1. Melt butter in large saucepan over medium heat. Add onion, celery and garlic. Cook and stir 5 minutes; place in slow cooker. Add broth, ham hock, beans and bay leaf. Cover; cook on HIGH 2 hours.

2. Remove ham hock; discard. Add potato and parsnip. Cover; cook 2 hours.

3. Add sausage. Cover; cook 30 minutes or until heated through. Remove and discard bay leaf. Season with salt and pepper. *Makes 6 to 8 servings*

Note: Use a 6-quart slow cooker for this recipe. If using a smaller slow cooker, cut the recipe ingredients in half.

2 tablespoons butter
1 large sweet onion, diced
3 stalks celery, diced
2 cloves garlic, chopped
8 cups chicken broth
1 ham hock
1½ cups dried red kidney beans, soaked in cold water 1 hour, drained and rinsed
1 bay leaf
1 sweet potato, diced
2 parsnips, diced
1 pound andouille smoked sausage or other pork sausage, cut into ½-inch pieces
Salt and black pepper

2 cans (15 ounces each) dark kidney beans, rinsed and drained
1 package (16 ounces) frozen bell pepper stir-fry mixture *or* 2 bell peppers*, chopped
1 cup frozen corn kernels
1 can (14½ ounces) diced tomatoes with peppers, celery and onions
3 tablespoons chili powder
2 teaspoons ground cumin, divided
2 teaspoons sugar
1 tablespoon extra virgin olive oil
½ teaspoon salt
Sour cream
Chopped cilantro

If using fresh bell peppers, add ½ cup chopped onion.

Double-Hearty, Double-Quick Veggie Chili

1. Combine beans, frozen pepper mixture, corn, tomatoes, chili powder, 1½ teaspoons cumin and sugar in slow cooker; mix well.

2. Cover; cook on LOW 5 hours or on HIGH 3 hours.

3. Stir in oil, salt and remaining ½ teaspoon cumin. Serve with sour cream and cilantro.
Makes 4 to 6 servings

Chilis & Soups

Potato and Leek Soup

1. Combine broth, potatoes, cabbage, leek, onion, carrots, parsley, salt, caraway seeds, pepper and bay leaf in slow cooker; mix well.

2. Cover; cook on LOW 8 to 10 hours or on HIGH 4 to 5 hours.

3. Remove and discard bay leaf. Combine ½ cup hot liquid from slow cooker and sour cream in small bowl. Add mixture and bacon to slow cooker; mix well.

Makes 6 to 8 servings

4 cups chicken broth
3 potatoes, peeled and diced
1½ cups chopped cabbage
1 leek, diced
1 onion, chopped
2 carrots, diced
¼ cup chopped fresh parsley
1 teaspoon salt
½ teaspoon caraway seeds
½ teaspoon black pepper
1 bay leaf
½ cup sour cream
1 pound bacon, crisp-cooked and crumbled

Cajun Chili

1½ pounds ground beef
2 cans (15 ounces each) Cajun-style mixed vegetables, undrained
2 cans (10¾ ounces each) condensed tomato soup
1 can (14½ ounces) diced tomatoes, undrained
3 sausages with Cheddar cheese (about 8 ounces), quartered and sliced into bite-size pieces
Shredded Cheddar cheese

1. Brown ground beef in large nonstick skillet over medium-high heat, stirring to separate meat. Drain and discard fat.

2. Place ground beef, mixed vegetables with juice, soup, tomatoes with juice and sausages in slow cooker.

3. Cover; cook on HIGH 2 to 3 hours. Serve with shredded cheese.

Makes 10 servings

Mediterranean Lentil Soup

1. Heat 2 tablespoons oil in large saucepan over medium heat. Add onion, celery and garlic; cook and stir 5 minutes. Stir in tomatoes, lentils, tomato paste and thyme. Combine lentil mixture, broth and bay leaves in slow cooker; mix well.

2. Cover; cook on LOW 8 hours or on HIGH 4 hours or until lentils are soft.

3. Meanwhile, prepare vinaigrette. Stir into soup just before serving. Season with salt and pepper.   *Makes 4 to 6 servings*

Vinaigrette: Combine ¾ cup packed fresh basil, ⅓ cup olive oil, 2 tablespoons minced fresh parsley and 2 tablespoons red wine vinegar in blender or food processor. Blend on high speed until smooth.

Note: Add 1 to 2 hours to cooking time if lentils are not soaked before cooking.

2 tablespoons olive oil
1 large sweet onion, diced
1 stalk celery, chopped
2 cloves garlic, minced
1 can (28 ounces) peeled whole plum tomatoes, drained and chopped
1½ cups dried lentils, soaked in cold water 1 hour, drained and rinsed
1 tablespoon tomato paste
1½ teaspoons dried thyme
6 cups beef broth
2 bay leaves
   Salt and black pepper

Vegetables & Sides

Garden Vegetable Tabbouleh Stew

1 large onion, chopped
2 medium carrots, cut into
 1-inch pieces
1 cup green beans, cut into
 1-inch pieces
2 medium green onions,
 thinly sliced
1 small zucchini, sliced
1 can (15 ounces)
 garbanzo beans
 (chick-peas), rinsed
 and drained
2 cans (14½ ounces each)
 diced tomatoes,
 undrained
¼ teaspoon salt
⅛ teaspoon black pepper
1 box (6 to 7 ounces)
 tabbouleh mix
1½ cups water
¼ cup olive oil
 Sour cream
 Chopped mint leaves

1. Layer onion, carrots, green beans, green onions, zucchini, chick-peas, tomatoes with juice, salt and pepper in slow cooker. Sprinkle tabbouleh mix over vegetables. Pour water and olive oil evenly over top.

2. Cover; cook on LOW 6 to 8 hours.

3. Serve with sour cream and mint.

Makes 4 servings

Donna's Potato Casserole

1 can (10¾ ounces)
    condensed cream
    of chicken soup
1 cup (8 ounces) sour
    cream
¼ cup chopped onion
¼ cup plus 3 tablespoons
    butter, melted and
    divided
1 teaspoon salt
2 pounds potatoes, peeled
    and chopped
2 cups (8 ounces) shredded
    Cheddar cheese
1½ to 2 cups stuffing mix

1. Combine soup, sour cream, onion, ¼ cup butter and salt in small bowl.

2. Combine potatoes and cheese in slow cooker. Pour soup mixture over potato mixture; mix well. Sprinkle stuffing mix over potato mixture; drizzle with remaining 3 tablespoons butter.

3. Cover; cook on LOW 8 to 10 hours or on HIGH 5 to 6 hours or until potatoes are tender. *Makes 8 to 10 servings*

Vegetables & Sides

Spicy Beans Tex-Mex

1. Boil lentils in water 20 to 30 minutes in large saucepan; drain. Cook bacon in medium skillet until crisp. Remove to paper towels; crumble bacon. Cook onion in same skillet in bacon drippings until soft.

2. Combine lentils, bacon, onion, beans, tomatoes with juice, ketchup, garlic, chili powder, cumin, pepper flakes and bay leaf in slow cooker.

3. Cover; cook on LOW 5 to 6 hours or on HIGH 3 to 4 hours. Remove and discard bay leaf before serving.

Makes 8 to 10 servings

⅓ cup lentils
1⅓ cups water
5 strips bacon
1 onion, chopped
1 can (15 ounces) pinto beans, undrained
1 can (15 ounces) red kidney beans, rinsed and drained
1 can (14½ ounces) diced tomatoes, undrained
3 tablespoons ketchup
3 cloves garlic, minced
1 teaspoon chili powder
½ teaspoon ground cumin
¼ teaspoon red pepper flakes
1 bay leaf

Mushroom Barley Stew

1 tablespoon olive oil
1 medium onion, finely chopped
1 cup chopped carrots (about 2 carrots)
1 clove garlic, minced
1 cup pearl barley
1 cup dried wild mushrooms, broken into pieces
1 teaspoon salt
½ teaspoon black pepper
½ teaspoon dried thyme
5 cups vegetable broth

1. Heat oil in medium skillet over medium-high heat. Add onion, carrots and garlic; cook and stir 5 minutes or until tender. Place in slow cooker.

2. Add barley, mushrooms, salt, pepper and thyme to slow cooker. Stir in broth.

3. Cover; cook on LOW 6 to 7 hours. Adjust seasonings.

Makes 4 to 6 servings

Variation: To turn this thick robust stew into a soup, add 2 to 3 additional cups of broth. Cook the same length of time.

Vegetables & Sides

Southwestern Stuffed Peppers

1. Cut thin slice off top of each bell pepper. Carefully remove seeds, leaving pepper whole.

2. Combine beans, cheese, salsa, corn, onions, rice, chili powder and cumin in medium bowl. Spoon filling evenly into each pepper. Place peppers in slow cooker.

3. Cover; cook on LOW 4 to 6 hours. Serve with sour cream.

Makes 4 servings

4 green bell peppers
1 can (15 ounces) black beans, rinsed and drained
1 cup (4 ounces) shredded Pepper-Jack cheese
¾ cup medium salsa
½ cup frozen corn
½ cup chopped green onions with tops
⅓ cup uncooked long grain rice
1 teaspoon chili powder
½ teaspoon ground cumin
Sour cream

Garden Potato Casserole

1¼ pounds baking potatoes, unpeeled, sliced
1 small red or green bell pepper, thinly sliced
¼ cup chopped onion
2 tablespoons butter, cut into bits, divided
½ teaspoon salt
½ teaspoon dried thyme
Black pepper
1 small yellow squash, thinly sliced
1 cup (4 ounces) shredded sharp Cheddar cheese

1. Place potatoes, bell pepper, onion, 1 tablespoon butter, salt, thyme and black pepper in slow cooker; mix well. Evenly layer squash over potato mixture; add remaining 1 tablespoon butter.

2. Cover; cook on LOW 7 hours or on HIGH 4 hours.

3. Remove potato mixture to serving bowl. Sprinkle with cheese; let stand 2 to 3 minutes or until cheese melts. *Makes 5 servings*

Winter Squash and Apples

1. Combine salt and pepper in small bowl; set aside.

2. Cut squash into 2-inch pieces; place in slow cooker. Add apples and onion. Sprinkle with salt mixture; stir well. Cover; cook on LOW 6 to 7 hours.

3. Just before serving, stir in butter and season with additional salt and pepper.

Makes 4 to 6 servings

Variation: Add ¼ to ½ cup brown sugar and ½ teaspoon cinnamon with butter; mix well.

1 teaspoon salt
½ teaspoon black pepper
1 butternut squash (about 2 pounds), peeled and seeded
2 apples, cored and cut into slices
1 medium onion, quartered and sliced
1½ tablespoons butter

Southwestern Corn and Beans

1 tablespoon olive oil
1 large onion, diced
1 jalapeño pepper*, diced
1 clove garlic, minced
2 cans (15 ounces) light
　　red kidney beans,
　　rinsed and drained
4 cups frozen corn, thawed
1 can (14½ ounces) diced
　　tomatoes, undrained
1 green bell pepper, cut
　　into 1-inch pieces
2 teaspoons chili powder
¾ teaspoon salt
½ teaspoon ground cumin
½ teaspoon black pepper

*Jalapeño peppers can sting and
irritate the skin; wear rubber gloves
when handling peppers and do not
touch eyes. Wash hands after handling.

1. Heat oil in medium skillet over medium heat. Add onion, jalapeño pepper and garlic; cook 5 minutes. Combine onion mixture, kidney beans, corn, tomatoes with juice, bell pepper, chili powder, salt, cumin and black pepper in slow cooker.

2. Cover; cook on LOW 7 to 8 hours or on HIGH 2 to 3 hours.

3. Serve with sour cream and black olives, if desired. *Makes 6 servings*

Serving Suggestion: For a party, spoon this colorful vegetarian dish into hollowed-out bell peppers or bread bowls.

Escalloped Corn

1. Heat butter in small saucepan over medium heat. Add onion; cook and stir 5 minutes or until tender. Add flour. Cook over medium heat 1 minute, stirring constantly. Stir in milk. Bring to a boil. Boil 1 minute or until thickened, stirring constantly.

2. Process 2 cups corn in food processor or blender until coarsely chopped. Combine milk mixture, chopped and whole corn, salt, dried thyme, pepper and nutmeg in slow cooker; mix well.

3. Cover; cook on LOW 3½ to 4 hours or until mixture is bubbly around edge. Garnish with fresh thyme.   *Makes 6 servings*

Variation: Add ½ cup (2 ounces) shredded Cheddar cheese and 2 tablespoons grated Parmesan cheese before serving; stir until melted. Garnish with additional shredded Cheddar cheese.

2 tablespoons butter
½ cup chopped onion
3 tablespoons all-purpose flour
1 cup milk
4 cups frozen corn, thawed, divided
½ teaspoon salt
½ teaspoon dried thyme
¼ teaspoon black pepper
⅛ teaspoon ground nutmeg
Fresh thyme

Vegetables & Sides

Cheesy Broccoli Casserole

2 packages (10 ounces each) chopped broccoli, thawed

1 can (10¾ ounces) condensed cream of potato soup

1¼ cups shredded sharp Cheddar cheese, divided

¼ cup minced onion

1 teaspoon hot pepper sauce

1 cup crushed potato chips or saltine crackers

1. Lightly grease slow cooker. Combine broccoli, soup, 1 cup cheese, onion and pepper sauce in slow cooker; mix well.

2. Cover; cook on LOW 5 to 6 hours or on HIGH 2½ to 3 hours.

3. Sprinkle top with crackers and remaining ½ cup cheese. Cook, uncovered, on LOW 30 to 60 minutes or until cheese melts.*   *Makes 4 to 6 servings*

For a crispy topping, transfer casserole to a baking dish. Sprinkle with remaining cheese and crackers; bake 5 to 10 minutes in preheated 400°F oven.

Cran-Orange Acorn Squash

1. Slice off tops of squash and enough of bottoms so squash will sit upright. Scoop out seeds and discard; set squash aside.

2. Combine rice, onion, celery, cranberries and sage in small bowl. Stuff each squash with rice mixture; dot with butter. Pour 1 tablespoon orange juice into each squash over stuffing. Stand squash in slow cooker. Pour water into bottom of slow cooker.

3. Cover; cook on LOW 2½ hours or until squash are tender.

Makes 6 servings

Tip: The skin of acorn squash is very tough. To make slicing easier, microwave the whole squash at HIGH 5 minutes to soften the skin.

3 **small acorn or carnival squash**
5 **tablespoons instant brown rice**
3 **tablespoons minced onion**
3 **tablespoons diced celery**
3 **tablespoons dried cranberries**
  Pinch ground or dried sage leaves
1 **teaspoon butter, cut into bits**
3 **tablespoons orange juice**
½ **cup water**

Sweet Potato & Pecan Casserole

1 can (40 ounces) sweet potatoes, drained and mashed
½ cup apple juice
⅓ cup plus 2 tablespoons butter, melted and divided
½ teaspoon salt
½ teaspoon ground cinnamon
¼ teaspoon black pepper
2 eggs, beaten
⅓ cup chopped pecans
⅓ cup brown sugar
2 tablespoons all-purpose flour

1. Lightly grease slow cooker. Combine sweet potatoes, apple juice, ⅓ cup butter, salt, cinnamon and pepper in large bowl. Beat in eggs. Place mixture into prepared slow cooker.

2. Combine pecans, brown sugar, flour and remaining 2 tablespoons butter in small bowl. Spread over sweet potatoes.

3. Cover; cook on HIGH 3 to 4 hours. *Makes 6 to 8 servings*

Note: This casserole is excellent to make for the holidays. Using the slow cooker frees the oven for other dishes.

Vegetables & Sides

Mexican-Style Rice and Cheese

1. Grease slow cooker well. Combine beans, tomatoes with juice, 1 cup cheese, rice, onion, cream cheese and garlic in slow cooker; mix well.

2. Cover; cook on LOW 6 to 9 hours.

3. Sprinkle with remaining 1 cup cheese just before serving.

Makes 6 to 8 servings

1 can (16 ounces) **red beans**
1 can (14½ ounces) **diced tomatoes with green chilies, undrained**
2 cups (8 ounces) **shredded Monterey Jack or Colby cheese, divided**
1½ cups **uncooked long-grain rice**
1 large **onion, finely chopped**
½ package (4 ounces) **cream cheese**
3 cloves **garlic, minced**

Rustic Cheddar Mashed Potatoes

2 pounds russet potatoes, peeled and diced
1 cup water
1/3 cup butter, cut into small pieces
1/2 to 3/4 cup milk
1 1/4 teaspoons salt
1/2 teaspoon black pepper
1/2 cup finely chopped green onions
1/2 to 3/4 cup (2 to 3 ounces) shredded Cheddar cheese

1. Combine potatoes and water in slow cooker; dot with butter. Cover; cook on LOW 6 hours or on HIGH 3 hours or until potatoes are tender.

2. Whip potatoes with electric mixer at medium speed until well blended. Add milk, salt and pepper; whip until well blended.

3. Stir in green onions and cheese. Cover; let stand 15 minutes to allow flavors to blend and cheese to melt. *Makes 8 servings*

Scalloped Potatoes and Parsnips

1. Melt butter in medium saucepan over medium-high heat. Add flour and whisk constantly 3 to 5 minutes. Slowly whisk in cream, mustard, salt, thyme and pepper. Stir until smooth.

2. Place potatoes, parsnips and onion in slow cooker. Add cream sauce.

3. Cover; cook on LOW 7 hours or on HIGH 3½ hours or until potatoes are tender. Stir in cheese. Cover; let stand until cheese melts.

Makes 4 to 6 servings

6 tablespoons butter

3 tablespoons all-purpose flour

1¾ cups heavy cream

2 teaspoons dry mustard

1½ teaspoons salt

1 teaspoon dried thyme

½ teaspoon black pepper

2 baking potatoes, cut in half lengthwise, then into ¼-inch slices

2 parsnips, cut into ¼-inch slices

1 onion, chopped

2 cups (8 ounces) shredded sharp Cheddar cheese

Risotto-Style Peppered Rice

1 cup uncooked long-grain
    rice
1 medium green bell
    pepper, chopped
1 medium red bell pepper,
    chopped
1 cup chopped onion
½ teaspoon ground
    turmeric
⅛ teaspoon ground red
    pepper
1 can (14½ ounces)
    chicken broth
1 cup (4 ounces) shredded
    Monterey Jack cheese
½ cup milk
¼ cup (½ stick) butter,
    cubed
1 teaspoon salt

1. Place rice, bell peppers, onion, turmeric and ground red pepper in slow cooker. Stir in broth.

2. Cover; cook on LOW 4 to 5 hours or until rice is done.

3. Stir in cheese, milk, butter and salt; fluff rice with fork. Cover; cook on LOW 5 minutes or until cheese melts.

Makes 4 to 6 servings

Caribbean Sweet Potato & Bean Stew

1. Combine sweet potatoes, beans, broth, onion, jerk seasoning, thyme, salt and cinnamon in slow cooker.

2. Cover; cook on LOW 5 to 6 hours or until vegetables are tender.

3. Adjust seasonings. Serve with almonds and hot pepper sauce.

Makes 4 servings

Tip: To toast almonds, spread in single layer on baking sheet. Bake in preheated 350°F oven 8 to 10 minutes or until golden brown, stirring frequently.

**2 medium sweet potatoes,
  peeled and cut into
  1-inch pieces
2 cups frozen cut green
  beans, thawed
1 can (15 ounces) black
  beans, rinsed and
  drained
1 can (14½ ounces)
  vegetable broth
1 small onion, sliced
2 teaspoons Caribbean or
  Jamaican jerk
  seasoning
½ teaspoon dried thyme
¼ teaspoon salt
¼ teaspoon ground
  cinnamon
⅓ cup slivered almonds,
  toasted
  Hot pepper sauce**

Spanish Paella-Style Rice

2 cans (14½ ounces each) chicken broth

1½ cups uncooked long - grain rice

1 small red bell pepper, diced

⅓ cup dry white wine or water

½ teaspoon powdered saffron *or* ½ teaspoon ground turmeric

⅛ teaspoon red pepper flakes

½ cup frozen peas, thawed

Salt

1. Combine broth, rice, bell pepper, wine, saffron and pepper flakes in slow cooker; mix well.

2. Cover; cook on LOW 4 hours or until liquid is absorbed.

3. Stir in peas. Cover; cook 15 to 30 minutes or until peas are hot. Season with salt.

Makes 6 servings

Variations: Add ½ cup cooked chicken, ham or shrimp or quartered marinated artichokes, drained, with peas.

Peasant Potatoes

1. Melt butter in large skillet over medium heat. Add onion and garlic. Cook and stir 5 minutes or until onion is transparent. Stir in sausage and oregano; cook 5 minutes. Stir in potatoes, salt and pepper; mix well. Transfer mixture to slow cooker.

2. Cover; cook on LOW 6 to 8 hours or on HIGH 3 to 4 hours, stirring every hour. Add cabbage and peppers during last 30 minutes of cooking,

3. Sprinkle with Parmesan cheese before serving.

Makes 6 servings

¼ cup (½ stick) butter
1 large sweet onion, chopped
2 cloves garlic, chopped
½ pound smoked beef sausage, cut into ¾-inch slices
1 teaspoon dried oregano
6 medium potatoes, preferably Yukon Gold, cut into 2-inch pieces
Salt and pepper
2 cups sliced cabbage
1 cup diced roasted red bell pepper
½ cup shaved fresh Parmesan cheese

Desserts

Cran-Apple Orange Conserve

2 medium oranges
5 large tart apples, peeled, cored and chopped
2 cups sugar
1½ cups fresh cranberries
1 tablespoon grated fresh lemon peel
Pound cake

1. Remove a thin slice from both ends of both oranges for easier chopping. Finely chop unpeeled oranges to make 2 cups chopped orange; remove any seeds. Combine oranges, apples, sugar, cranberries and lemon peel in slow cooker. Cover; cook on HIGH 4 hours. Slightly crush fruit with potato masher.

2. Cook, uncovered, on LOW 4 hours or on HIGH 2 to 2½ hours or until very thick, stirring occasionally to prevent sticking.

3. Cool at least 2 hours. Serve with pound cake. *Makes about 5 cups*

Serving Suggestion: Fruit conserve can also be served with roast pork or poultry.

1½ cups milk
3 eggs
½ cup sugar
3 tablespoons dark rum
    or milk
⅛ teaspoon salt
1 medium banana, sliced
    ¼ inch thick
15 to 18 vanilla wafers

Banana-Rum Custard
with Vanilla Wafers

1. Beat milk, eggs, sugar, rum and salt in medium bowl. Pour into 1-quart casserole. Do not cover.

2. Add rack to 5-quart slow cooker and pour in 1 cup water. Place casserole on rack. Cover; cook on LOW 3½ to 4 hours.

3. Remove casserole from slow cooker. Spoon custard into individual dessert dishes. Arrange banana slices and wafers over custard. Garnish as desired.

Makes 5 servings

Decadent Chocolate Delight

1. Lightly grease inside of slow cooker.

2. Combine cake mix, sour cream, chocolate chips, water, eggs, oil and pudding and pie filling mix in slow cooker; mix well.

3. Cover; cook on LOW 6 to 8 hours or on HIGH 3 to 4 hours. Serve hot or warm with ice cream.

Makes 12 servings

1 package (about 18 ounces) chocolate cake mix
1 cup (8 ounces) sour cream
1 cup chocolate chips
1 cup water
4 eggs
¾ cup vegetable oil
1 package (4-serving size) instant chocolate pudding and pie filling mix

Desserts

Luscious Pecan Bread Pudding

3 cups French bread cubes

3 tablespoons chopped
    pecans, toasted

2¼ cups milk

2 eggs, beaten

½ cup sugar

1 teaspoon vanilla

¾ teaspoon ground
    cinnamon, divided

¾ cup cranberry juice
    cocktail

1½ cups frozen pitted tart
    cherries

2 tablespoons sugar
    substitute

1. Toss bread cubes and pecans in soufflé dish. Combine milk, eggs, sugar, vanilla and ½ teaspoon cinnamon in large bowl. Pour over bread mixture in soufflé dish. Cover tightly with foil. Make foil handles (see note). Place soufflé dish on top of foil strips in slow cooker. Pour hot water into slow cooker to about 1½ inches from top of soufflé dish. Cover; cook on LOW 2 to 3 hours.

2. Meanwhile, combine cranberry juice and remaining ¼ teaspoon cinnamon in small saucepan; stir in frozen cherries. Bring sauce to a boil over medium heat; cook 5 minutes. Remove from heat. Stir in sugar substitute.

3. Lift soufflé dish from slow cooker with foil handles. Serve bread pudding with cherry sauce. *Makes 6 servings*

Foil Handles: Tear off three 18×2-inch strips of heavy foil or use regular foil folded to double thickness. Crisscross foil strips in spoke design and place in slow cooker to allow for easy removal of bread pudding.

Tart Cherries

Cherry Flan

1. Grease inside of slow cooker.

2. Beat eggs, sugar and salt in large bowl of electric mixer at high speed until thick. Add flour; beat until smooth. Beat in evaporated milk and vanilla.

3. Pour batter into prepared slow cooker. Place cherries evenly over batter. Cover; cook on LOW 3½ to 4 hours or until flan is set. Serve warm with whipped cream. *Makes 6 servings*

Note: This yummy dessert is best served warm and is especially delicious when topped with whipped cream or ice cream.

5 **eggs**
½ **cup sugar**
½ **teaspoon salt**
¾ **cup flour**
1 **can (12 ounces)
    evaporated milk**
1 **teaspoon vanilla**
1 **bag (16 ounces) frozen,
    pitted dark sweet
    cherries, thawed**
  **Sweetened whipped
    cream or cherry vanilla
    ice cream**

Chocolate Croissant Pudding

1½ cups milk
3 eggs
½ cup sugar
¼ cup unsweetened cocoa powder
½ teaspoon vanilla
¼ teaspoon salt
2 plain croissants, cut into 1-inch pieces
½ cup chocolate chips
Whipped cream

1. Beat milk, eggs, sugar, cocoa, vanilla and salt in medium bowl.

2. Grease 1-quart casserole. Layer half the croissants, chocolate chips and half the egg mixture in casserole. Repeat layers with remaining croissants and egg mixture.

3. Add rack to 5-quart slow cooker; pour in 1 cup water. Place casserole on rack. Cover; cook on LOW 3 to 4 hours. Remove casserole from slow cooker. Serve pudding with whipped cream.

Makes 6 servings

Baked Ginger Apples

1. Slice tops off apples; core. Combine butter, nuts, apricots, ginger and brown sugar in medium bowl. Fill apples with nut mixture. Place apples in slow cooker. Pour brandy into slow cooker. Cover; cook on LOW 4 hours or on HIGH 2 hours.

2. Gently remove apples from slow cooker; keep warm. Combine pudding mix and cream in small bowl. Add to slow cooker; stir to combine with brandy. Cover; cook on HIGH 30 minutes. Stir until smooth. Return apples to slow cooker; keep warm until ready to serve.

3. Serve apples with cream mixture.

Makes 4 servings

4 large Red Delicious apples
½ cup (1 stick) unsalted butter, melted
⅓ cup chopped macadamia nuts
¼ cup chopped dried apricots
2 tablespoons finely chopped crystallized ginger
1 tablespoon dark brown sugar
¾ cup brandy
½ cup vanilla pudding and pie filling mix
2 cups heavy cream

Steamed Southern Sweet Potato Custard

1 can (16 ounces) cut sweet potatoes, drained
1 can (12 ounces) evaporated milk, divided
½ cup packed light brown sugar
2 eggs, lightly beaten
1 teaspoon ground cinnamon
½ teaspoon ground ginger
¼ teaspoon salt
Whipped cream
Ground nutmeg

1. Process sweet potatoes with ¼ cup milk in food processor or blender until smooth. Add remaining milk, brown sugar, eggs, cinnamon, ginger and salt; process until well mixed. Pour into ungreased 1-quart soufflé dish. Cover tightly with foil. Crumple large sheet (about 15×12 inches) of foil; place in bottom of slow cooker. Pour 2 cups water over foil. Make foil handles (see note). Place soufflé dish on top of foil strips in slow cooker.

2. Cover; cook on HIGH 2½ to 3 hours or until skewer inserted in center comes out clean.

3. Using foil strips, lift dish from slow cooker; transfer to wire rack. Uncover; let stand 30 minutes. Garnish with whipped cream and nutmeg.

Makes 4 servings

Foil Handles: Tear off three 18×2-inch strips of heavy foil or use regular foil folded to double thickness. Crisscross foil strips in spoke design; place in slow cooker to allow for easy removal of custard.

Desserts

Mixed Berry Cobbler

1. Stir together berries, granulated sugar, tapioca and lemon peel in slow cooker.

2. Combine flour, brown sugar, baking powder and nutmeg in medium bowl. Add milk and butter; stir just until blended. Drop spoonfuls on top of berry mixture.

3. Cover; cook on LOW 4 hours. Uncover; let stand about 30 minutes. Serve with ice cream.

Makes 8 servings

1 package (16 ounces) frozen mixed berries
¾ cup granulated sugar
2 tablespoons quick-cooking tapioca
2 teaspoons grated fresh lemon peel
1½ cups all-purpose flour
½ cup packed brown sugar
2¼ teaspoons baking powder
¼ teaspoon ground nutmeg
¾ cup milk
⅓ cup butter, melted
Ice cream

Baked Fudge Pudding Cake

6 tablespoons unsweetened cocoa powder
¼ cup all-purpose flour
⅛ teaspoon salt
4 eggs
1⅓ cups sugar
1 cup (2 sticks) unsalted butter, melted
1 teaspoon vanilla
Grated peel of 1 orange
½ cup heavy cream
Chopped toasted pecans, whipped cream or vanilla ice cream

1. Spray inside of slow cooker with nonstick cooking spray. Preheat slow cooker on LOW setting. Combine cocoa, flour and salt in small bowl; set aside.

2. Beat eggs with electric mixer on medium-high speed until thickened. Gradually add sugar; beat 5 minutes or until very thick and lemon-colored. Mix in butter, vanilla and peel. Stir cocoa mixture into egg mixture. Add heavy cream; mix until combined. Pour batter into slow cooker.

3. Before placing lid on slow cooker, cover opening with a paper towel to collect condensation, making sure it does not touch the pudding mixture. (Large slow cookers might require 2 connected paper towels.) Place lid over paper towel. Cook on LOW 3 to 4 hours. (Do not cook on HIGH.) Sprinkle with pecans; serve with whipped cream. Refrigerate leftovers.

Makes 6 to 8 servings

Note: Store leftover cake in a covered container in the refrigerator. To serve leftover cake, reheat individual servings in the microwave for about 15 seconds. Or, make Baked Fudge Truffles: roll leftover cake into small balls and dip them into melted chocolate. Let sit until chocolate hardens.

Index

Metric Conversion Chart

VOLUME MEASUREMENTS (dry)

$\frac{1}{8}$ teaspoon = 0.5 mL
$\frac{1}{4}$ teaspoon = 1 mL
$\frac{1}{2}$ teaspoon = 2 mL
$\frac{3}{4}$ teaspoon = 4 mL
1 teaspoon = 5 mL
1 tablespoon = 15 mL
2 tablespoons = 30 mL
$\frac{1}{4}$ cup = 60 mL
$\frac{1}{3}$ cup = 75 mL
$\frac{1}{2}$ cup = 125 mL
$\frac{2}{3}$ cup = 150 mL
$\frac{3}{4}$ cup = 175 mL
1 cup = 250 mL
2 cups = 1 pint = 500 mL
3 cups = 750 mL
4 cups = 1 quart = 1 L

VOLUME MEASUREMENTS (fluid)

1 fluid ounce (2 tablespoons) = 30 mL
4 fluid ounces ($\frac{1}{2}$ cup) = 125 mL
8 fluid ounces (1 cup) = 250 mL
12 fluid ounces ($1\frac{1}{2}$ cups) = 375 mL
16 fluid ounces (2 cups) = 500 mL

WEIGHTS (mass)

$\frac{1}{2}$ ounce = 15 g
1 ounce = 30 g
3 ounces = 90 g
4 ounces = 120 g
8 ounces = 225 g
10 ounces = 285 g
12 ounces = 360 g
16 ounces = 1 pound = 450 g

DIMENSIONS

$\frac{1}{16}$ inch = 2 mm
$\frac{1}{8}$ inch = 3 mm
$\frac{1}{4}$ inch = 6 mm
$\frac{1}{2}$ inch = 1.5 cm
$\frac{3}{4}$ inch = 2 cm
1 inch = 2.5 cm

OVEN TEMPERATURES

250°F = 120°C
275°F = 140°C
300°F = 150°C
325°F = 160°C
350°F = 180°C
375°F = 190°C
400°F = 200°C
425°F = 220°C
450°F = 230°C

BAKING PAN SIZES

Utensil	Size in Inches/Quarts	Metric Volume	Size in Centimeters
Baking or Cake Pan (square or rectangular)	8×8×2	2 L	20×20×5
	9×9×2	2.5 L	23×23×5
	12×8×2	3 L	30×20×5
	13×9×2	3.5 L	33×23×5
Loaf Pan	8×4×3	1.5 L	20×10×7
	9×5×3	2 L	23×13×7
Round Layer Cake Pan	8×1½	1.2 L	20×4
	9×1½	1.5 L	23×4
Pie Plate	8×1¼	750 mL	20×3
	9×1¼	1 L	23×3
Baking Dish or Casserole	1 quart	1 L	—
	1½ quart	1.5 L	—
	2 quart	2 L	—

Metric Conversion Chart